Praise for *Experience Is Everything*

"Jeannie makes CX feel doable, disciplined, and downright energizing! Jeannie doesn't just talk about customer experience—she shows you how to build it into your muscles. Her microhabits hit that sweet spot where mindset meets discipline, turning everyday moments into compounding growth. This is the kind of book you finish and immediately think, 'Oh…I can use this Monday.' And then you actually do."
—**HENNA PRYOR**, CSP, Speaker, Bestselling Author, *Inc.* Writer

"Nobody understands daily customer moments better than Jeannie—this book shows leaders how to design them intentionally and deliver them consistently."
—**ADAM TOPOREK**, Author of *Be Your Customer's Hero*

"This book turns engagement theory into daily CX practice. Follow Jeannie's steps and watch morale and loyalty climb together."
—**JOE MULL**, Author of *Employalty* and Founder, Boss Hero

"Jeannie shows leaders how to show up for customers with the same credibility she models onstage—intentional, authentic, and consistently customer-first. Jeannie's years of experience and passion for her work is hands down brilliant, and her concepts work! She has consistently demonstrated what she recommends for her clients through the top-notch customer experience she delivers."

—**STACEY HANKE,** CEO and Keynote Speaker

"Built on integrity and practical insight, Jeannie shows how small, intentional moments create big wins. Delaware North has seen it firsthand."

—**MARCUS STORY,** Senior Director, Customer Experience, Delaware North

"Jeannie Walters doesn't just talk about customer experience—she makes it actionable, human, and (above all) doable. *Experience Is Everything* proves that CX isn't a department—it's a discipline. Essential reading for every CX leader."

—**ANN HANDLEY,** Bestselling Author and Chief Content Officer, MarketingProfs

"Packed with practical ideas and memorable stories, *Experience Is Everything* shows you how to create intentional moments of magic at scale. If you want customer experience to be your competitive edge, read this book before your competitors do."

—**SHEP HYKEN,** CX Expert and *New York Times* Bestselling Author of *The Amazement Revolution*

"This is an incredibly useful, practical, and clear playbook for demystifying experiences and turning them into a powerful business advantage. Highly recommended for all business leaders who care about customers."

—**JAY BAER,** Author of *The Time to Win: How to Exceed Your Customers' Need for Speed* and *New York Times* Bestselling Author

"For years, I've watched Jeannie turn empathy and clarity into real, consistent customer experiences. This book is the antidote to performative 'We care about customers' slides—finally giving leaders a way to prove it in every moment."

—**GINI DIETRICH,** Founder and CEO, Spin Sucks and Creator, PESO Model®

"With trademark integrity and decades-deep CX expertise, Jeannie shows why disciplined customer experience isn't soft—it's a truly winning strategy in any business. Get ready to build your own CX Mission Statement and turn ideas into real outcomes."

—**SID BANERJEE,** Chief Strategy Officer, Medallia

EXPERIENCE IS EVERYTHING

MAKING EVERY MOMENT COUNT
IN THE AGE OF CUSTOMER EXPECTATIONS

JEANNIE WALTERS

Experience Is Everything:
Making Every Moment Count in the Age of Customer Expectations

Copyright © 2026 by Jeannie Walters

All rights reserved. No part of this publication may be reproduced, stored in a retrieval system, or transmitted in any form by any means, electronic, mechanical, photocopy, recording, or otherwise, without the prior permission of the publisher, except as provided by USA copyright law.

No patent liability is assumed with respect to the use of the information contained herein. Although every precaution has been taken in the preparation of this book, the publisher and author assume no responsibility for errors or omissions. Neither is any liability assumed for damages resulting from the use of the information contained herein.

Published by Mission Driven Press, an imprint of Forefront Books, Nashville, Tennessee.
Distributed by Simon & Schuster.

Library of Congress Control Number: 2025927573

Print ISBN: 978-1-63763-446-2
E-book ISBN: 978-1-63763-447-9

Cover Design by George Stevens, G Sharp Design LLC
Interior Design by Bill Kersey, KerseyGraphics

Printed in the United States of America

26 27 28 29 30 31 [RR4] 10 9 8 7 6 5 4 3 2 1

CONTENTS

Acknowledgments 9

Introduction: CX 11

Chapter 1: Crafting the CX Mission Statement 21

Chapter 2: Create the Mindset—
Using Your CX Mission Statement 57

Chapter 3: Customer Experience Is a Strategy—
Defining Your CX Success Blueprint. 69

Chapter 4: Know Your Customer's True Journey—
The Customer Journey Map 97

Chapter 5: A CX Culture. 147

Chapter 6: Building New Habits . . . as a Team 179

Chapter 7: A CX Charter of Your Own. 193

Conclusion 211

What's Next?. 215

Notes 217

One Last Thing 219

ACKNOWLEDGMENTS

Experience Is Everything is here after more than two decades working with leaders who want to deliver meaningful experiences to those around them. These leaders, whether they have "customer experience" in their title or not, are seeking ways to balance creating easier, faster, more pleasant experiences with the real-world demands of business results. I've been honored to work alongside some of the most thoughtful and dedicated leaders out there. I remain honored to be part of their journey. This book is for them.

I'm also extraordinarily fortunate to have a robust cheering section, which helps me believe I can do things like start a business, speak to audiences around the world, and write a book that people will read. That support is the foundation of everything I do.

My husband and I raised two extraordinary people, who are now young adults, while I was growing my business. Our family has juggled schedules, put up with early trips to the airport, and seen me through the highs and lows of being an entrepreneur. I'm forever grateful. Mike, Savannah, and Nolan, I love you more than I can express.

ACKNOWLEDGMENTS

That foundation of support was laid early. Mom and Dad, thank you for always believing in us by letting us be who we were going to be. To my siblings, Dave, Bill, Patty, and Bob, along with my in-laws and my amazing nieces and nephews, I'm so grateful for sharing this journey with you.

There are simply too many other members of my communities to name. The pioneers of CX I'm lucky to call friends, my speaker community, those digital marketing friends who've ridden this wave with me... you've inspired me.

To my teams. Experience Investigators is home to talented and dedicated people who have helped me get here. And my book team, including Chris Murray, Zachary Gresham, Larissa Salazer, and the entire team at Brand Builders Group, thanks for turning this idea into a reality.

And finally, to you, the reader. This book is meant to be optimistic. I hope it serves you well as you create experiences that are more empathetic, meaningful, and human for all of us.

INTRODUCTION

CX

CUSTOMER EXPERIENCE.

Those two words can evoke several definitions, depending on who you ask.

People love to conflate the idea of customer experience—or *CX*—with customer service. What's the difference? Well, let's talk about it.

Customer experience is what happens between a brand and a customer along every step of their journey: that means each interaction, each touchpoint, each communication. These experiences lead to a perception by the customer. Was that better than expected? Worse? Surprising? Memorable? Meaningful?

Customer service, however, is what happens when customers need support, service, or information. Customer service is an important part of the overall customer experience... but it's not the only part.

I like to make this distinction: Customer experience is *proactive*. Customer service is *reactive*.

INTRODUCTION

And my first ask of you, my new CX friend, is for you to approach the ideas in this book *proactively*. You are in control and empowered to consider, design, and deliver the customer experience. You are allowed to think big. You are going to approach your role here not as a passive reader but as a powerful customer experience change agent!

Deal?

Great. We're friends already.

I like to think about CX as a relationship. Years ago, when our kids were little, we experienced a true moment within a customer experience. My son has a tree-nut allergy. These types of allergies are very serious. He carries medicine and an EpiPen wherever he goes. When he was in grade school, we had to replenish the supply of EpiPens every year, as the medicine expires. You'll notice I say *pens*, plural. We needed to have one for the school nurse, for the babysitter, for the car, for the downstairs bathroom and the upstairs bathroom, for the soccer bag, and for the backpack. I can't recall how many we actually got, but it was quite a few each year.

Well, one year the price skyrocketed. Each EpiPen was now around $1,800. This was devastating news to us, of course, but my husband and I determined that it was one of those expenses we couldn't avoid. We simply had to do it.

We have used the same local pharmacy for many years. We submitted our massive EpiPen order to them, as usual.

Later that day, they called. The head pharmacist said he was upset and angry about the price hike. One of the big pharmacy chains had announced a special coupon to combat that pricing. This small, local pharmacy couldn't compete, but he had sent my prescription there with the coupon. It saved us thousands of dollars and cost our pharmacy even more in lost business.

I continue to share this story, years later, because it's such an excellent example of proactive customer experience. Instead of just reacting with a "What are you gonna do?" attitude, this small business understood the value of a long-term customer. They thought beyond the transaction and focused on the relationship.

This is what you and I need to do in leading customer experience.

I'm Talking to You

You might be reading this and thinking, *We sell whatsits*, or *I work in a government agency*, or simply, *This doesn't apply to me.*

Oh, but it does. We have customer experiences when we are going to a Beyoncé concert or paying a parking ticket. In each case, we have a goal as a customer, and we want to achieve that goal in the easiest, most convenient, and most delightful way possible.

Yet customer experience can't be just about the customers. That sounds weird, I know! But most of us are here to deliver on a job. We have businesses to run, goals to achieve, and outcomes to report. That means we have to approach CX as we approach any other part of the business; it's about balancing the efforts we put into the experience for customers with the outcomes we want for our organizations.

In working with dozens of organizations (including financial services, retail, fitness, technology, government, nonprofit, education, health care, and more!), I've recognized a pattern among those who understood how to get the results they wanted out of the efforts they took. It came down to three things:

1. **A universal and defined customer experience mindset.** That's why we developed the CX Mission Statement as a standard. This can't be all talk—it becomes the North Star and vision for your customer experience. This is shared throughout the organization and used as a powerful tool to help everyone get aligned.
2. **A defined strategy.** This is the missing piece in most organizations. Without a defined strategy—a plan to achieve specific outcomes—everything feels ad hoc and disjointed. Your organization can't be all things to all people. This strategy helps define what you prioritize and why.
3. **The daily discipline to track progress and course correct.** Instead of focusing on vagaries or reacting to every fire drill, this requires the business acumen to align your efforts back to the mindset and strategy you have defined.

INTRODUCTION

Many organizations don't have a leader focused on customer experience. That might be your situation. But by picking up this book, you are telling me something about yourself. You understand the importance of customer experience. You see that it can be a winning business strategy when approached in this way. And you're ready to lead. You are a CX change agent.

CX as Your Organizing Principle

The success of your organization relies on some basic business realities.

You have to be profitable.
This is true for nonprofits and government agencies and everyone else. Your organizational budget has to be funded positively. This means we have to ensure that more revenue is coming into the organization than is going out in expenses. A positive, proactive customer experience can drive that profitability... but only if you know what goals to prioritize and how to put in the right efforts to achieve those goals.

You have to be efficient.
Even if the revenue is coming in, you have to manage expenses and reduce inefficiencies. This shows up in many ways. Poor customer experiences lead to organizational inefficiencies because they lead to reduced customer lifetime values, customer refunds, and higher service costs, to name just a few consequences.

INTRODUCTION

You have to have a great culture with happy employees. No organization will survive with employees who aren't happy. Our workplace cultures must reflect who we are and who we want to be. Employees need to feel empowered to take action that makes sense both for customers and for the organization overall. Consider approaching CX as an umbrella term that covers not just how we treat customers but also how we treat each other, how we treat partners and suppliers, and how we can all benefit from this approach. It's important to see CX as more of a total experience. In all its simplicity as a term, it is more nuanced and complex than most give it credit for.

Here We Go

In my work as a customer experience adviser, I partner with leaders just like you. These folks are often tapped on the shoulder and told, "Congratulations! You are now in charge of customer experience!" They're given little direction and fewer resources. Yet they know there is work to be done. They send out the surveys and see the negative feedback. They witness the siloed communications and broken processes and understand why customers feel neglected, frustrated, and disappointed. Yet they don't quite know what to do or where to start.

Or maybe the customer experience is going just fine—at least that's what the C-suite believes. And yet those in charge think more people in the company simply need to "get it." This is when the work can be especially challenging.

INTRODUCTION

My job includes sharing the hard truths. Your best, most loved customers love you back. But the majority feel neglected and ignored. And yes, your people need to "get it," but we have to spend some time defining what "it" means for your brand and organization.

I essentially see the work I do as education first, with a lot of empathy and compassion for the earnest leaders doing their best in often less-than-ideal circumstances. This is why I'm passionate about speaking, consulting, training, and writing around this topic.

With teaching in mind, we have developed a framework around the ideas that help make customer experience efforts succeed.

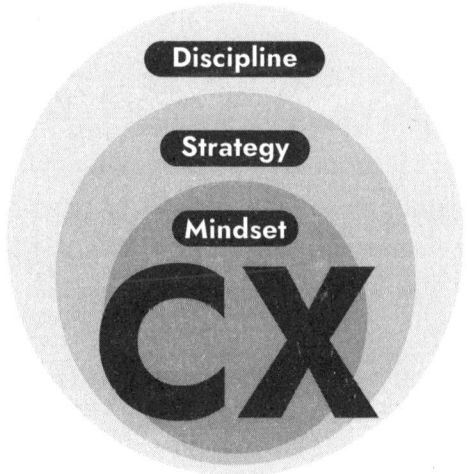

CX Foundations

INTRODUCTION

I believe we make this world a better place when we strive to do this well. The mission of my company, Experience Investigators, is "To create fewer ruined days for customers." It sounds deceptively simple, doesn't it? But it means we are removing points of friction from someone's day. We are focusing on the human we're serving and their real life, not some generic persona. We're helping them achieve their goal in a more convenient and delightful way. That's meaningful work. As you approach your role as a leader, I encourage you to think about that person.

The Crane on the Cover

At Experience Investigators, our logo—affectionately known as Craney—is more than a design; it's a symbol of purpose. Inspired by the Japanese tradition of folding paper cranes, which represent peace, healing, and hope, Craney reminds us that meaningful experiences are created through intention and care. In Japan, folding a thousand cranes is an act of patience and compassion—each fold a quiet promise to do something good for another. That practice mirrors how great customer experiences are built: not all at once, but moment by moment, through empathy and consistent action.

Craney also reflects the foundations of our work: mindset, strategy, and discipline.

INTRODUCTION

Craney

The mindset to approach every interaction with empathy. The strategy to connect those actions to a greater purpose. And the discipline to keep showing up—to listen, to act, and to serve—even when no one is watching. Each "fold" in that process represents a choice to make CX more human, more compassionate, and more impactful. Like Craney, when we bring heart and intention to our work, we create experiences that lift others—and help all of us rise together.

Let's make the world a better place, shall we?

CHAPTER 1

CRAFTING THE CX MISSION STATEMENT

A CUSTOMER-CENTERED MINDSET IS A CRITICAL PART OF defining a customer experience culture. I often see leaders make assumptions about this. They believe CX is "common sense" or simply ask employees to "think of the customer." But every person in your organization brings unique backgrounds, life experiences, and understanding. It's not fair to assume that what you believe to be a "great" customer experience is the same as what others believe.

So how do organizations overcome this? They align around one single idea of what the customer experience is. To facilitate this, we use a CX Mission Statement to create and reinforce that alignment.

The CX Mission Statement

The CX Mission Statement is a succinct, one- or two-sentence statement that captures the experience you want to create for every customer, every time. Regardless of industry or activity area; regardless of whether your organization is

B2B, B2C, or a nonprofit; and regardless of who your customers might be, the goal of this CX Mission Statement is the same: to provide your employees a consistent philosophy around what the customer experience should be and how all your employees—customer-facing or not—contribute to ensuring that customers are living the intended experience. It's about your promise. How can you show up for your customers consistently?

Developing and articulating the CX Mission Statement takes place through four key steps:

1. **Collect:** The first step is to take stock of where the organization stands *today* in terms of its overall vision, value, and mission. Do this by collecting these relevant documents, such as your organizational vision, mission, and values statements, and also speaking with key leaders and influencers within the organization in case there's something else floating around.
2. **Reflect:** Through four powerful questions, reflect on the experience your customers are promised and the experience you can *realistically* and consistently deliver.
3. **Connect:** Put it all together! Draw from the documents collected and the answers to the four reflection questions to craft the final words of the CX Mission Statement. Our CX Mission Statement template will help you structure this short yet

mobilizing declaration of your customer experience mission.

4. **Direct:** What's the use of a statement if it's never put into action? The CX Mission Statement is not merely a document but a tool to use. This final phase of the CX Mission Statement process is when you use the mission statement as a guide for every facet of your organizational activities.

STEP ONE: COLLECT

The first step in developing your CX Mission Statement is to collect information. The material that already exists in your organization can help you identify your organization's customer experience mission. The CX Mission Statement must reflect *who you are* as an organization and *how you want to show up for your customers*. You therefore want to collect anything that can shed any light on what makes your organization unique and that identifies the core ideas behind the customer relationships you want to build and the image you want to project.

Start by collecting documents such as your organization's mission, values, and vision statements and any other statements or declarations—at the corporate level but also at lower levels (like business units or departments) if such statements exist—related to customer experience. The actual names of the documents are irrelevant, since different companies will use different names. This may make them tricky to parse. Some companies, for example, use *layers* of documents. At the organizational level will be the corporate mission statement and perhaps a big value statement; at lower levels of the organization, you will find teams with their own mission statements or business units with vision statements. Some organizations keep a vision document and a set of twenty-five values. Keep your wits about you as you dig.

It's great if you can include your brand documents—like your brand promise, if that exists. It's okay if you don't come away with a perfect set of applicable documents. Collect what you can. What you're trying to do is make sure you start from a place that doesn't conflict with what is already defined about who you are as an organization.

Sometimes you may have to reach out to different leaders and ask guidance on where to find things. This can be a great way to build relationships and remind your leaders that customer experience is a focus. Many clients have shared that the discussions around values and how they should apply to CX have been powerful in connecting with leaders across their organizations. Be brave and ask for help! Take notes on what they tell you—sometimes that can help with mission statement development too.

Again, the names of the documents don't matter. The quantity of documents doesn't matter. If you only have a mission statement but no documents concerning values or laying out a vision, that's okay. Even if you find only one thing—that's okay. Just document what you can.

CHAPTER 1

The following ideas can guide you as you engage in your collection efforts. The first thing to recognize is that your first draft is going to be messy and disorganized. That's how first drafts are. Remember, keep your WHY front of mind. This is about delivering for your customers consistently and defining the expectations for everyone. It will be worth the work.

Does This Apply to Customers?

The core question to ask as you collect these documents is this: What best applies to customer experience? The important thing is that the documents you collect help reveal the aspirations and goals of the organization for its customers—even if the documents don't directly address the customer, as many don't.

Some of the existing statements you collect may be full of corporate speak (corporate mission statements are guilty of this!), but they can still be valuable. Look beyond the language and try to determine the core message: What are the authors of the statement in question really trying to get at here?

It's possible that you will review the documents you've collected and think, *None of this really applies to customer experience*. For example, you may find that your mission and vision statements aren't really about customers at all; they are about shareholder value or being "best in class." Many of these documents will be about big, grandiose ideas. All of that is great for two reasons. First, because you are going to take these big, grandiose ideas and look for the motivations behind the words. And second, because you want to make sure that you are not writing a CX Mission Statement that conflicts with those motivations. The goal in this process is to make sure that you're building on whatever exists in your organization already.

Sometimes, you get lucky! Every so often, an organization's vision or mission statement is quite good and applies directly to the customer experience. Great! You will be able to take much of that content as a jumping-off point for the CX Mission Statement. On even rarer occasions, you can use your organizational mission statement *as* your CX Mission Statement. . . . But I'll be honest—I haven't seen many examples that are perfect fits.

You will also have to turn on your discernment, because there may be some universal truths or assumptions about the organization's values and mission that are not necessarily documented. Undocumented truths about customer experience present an opportunity for the CX Mission Statement to clarify and make explicit what many people know already. For example, your CEO might talk about treating customers like family. That's significant when it comes to customer experience. Use what you know about what's important to your organization and leaders, even if it's not black-and-white.

Acknowledge What's There and Stick to the Script
As you collect nuggets from the extant documents, don't be afraid to summarize. Sometimes you will be given

very lengthy documents with a bit too much information. Summarize this information to focus on the core ideas that you want to make sure will be included in the CX Mission Statement. Remember, it's not about perfection; it's about progress. (I often remind my clients of this with a mantra: Progress over Perfection!)

On the other hand, if you're having trouble finding enough documentation, you may be tempted to create some documentation yourself. For example, you might think, *We often talk about being service-minded* or *We're really about showing up for the customer as gracious hosts*. Jot that stuff down, but keep it separate; in this phase, you are collecting what exists. Riffing too early creates the risk of undermining the organization's mission.

Likewise, don't change anything that already exists. You might be tempted to adjust a document's text to make it mesh more closely with the idea of customer experience. Or you might be tempted to adjust the phrasing or change some words because you feel the words are just "not right" or you want to go in a different direction. Remember that in the collection phase, you want to make sure that you're representing the truth of your organization *today*.

The bottom line: It's absolutely vital to acknowledge and respect what is valuable to you and your organization today. To do otherwise will invite pushback when you roll out the CX Mission Statement later. People will look at the CX Mission Statement and think, *This doesn't reflect our* values at all. Our values include _____. Why don't they have _____ in the CX Mission Statement?

More Voices

One of the biggest challenges for any CX leader is getting leadership and cross-functional buy-in. That is why—in every step of the process, starting with collecting and including reflecting, connecting, and (as we will see in the next chapter) directing—you want to bring in other people from your organization. This is the only way to get buy-in from throughout the organization from the beginning. To meet this challenge, you have to consistently and continuously make sure you're including others, you're collecting opinions, and you're respecting those opinions. Acknowledging and respecting the opinions of others helps to gain their buy-in. After all, those who help you build the CX Mission Statement will not come at you when you're rolling it out. You don't want people claiming you've ignored key elements of the mission, vision, or values that already existed in the organization.

At least a little bit of "Hey, what about this?" pushback is going to happen, especially concerning ideals or values that are not formally documented. Enlisting others is the most important way to keep that kind of pushback under control. If someone says you missed something, you can list the key people throughout the organization that you included in the process and explain how the CX Mission Statement reflects their opinions. You can likewise respond to those who might object to non-formally documented ideals or values that are included in the statement. Categorize those opinions and thoughts as *what we hear* or *what we know*, and keep a list of the people you and your team talked to throughout the organization.

Your CX Mission Statement might look like change to employees. They might resist the idea of documenting what they feel they do as "common sense," or they might view the documentation as more work for them. Embrace those potential naysayers early by including them in the collection process. Help them feel engaged and invested from the start so they can help champion the result.

Too Many Chefs?

At the same time—and this is the balance you have to achieve as you craft the CX Mission Statement—please don't invite too many people to the table. This is tricky because there is no magic number. Consider people who have real influence. This may include leaders who have authority and accountability around real change at your organization as well as those cross-functional managers who understand customers. Include these people. Their involvement will help you collect information and will ensure that you will have their buy-in and backing when your CX Mission Statement rolls out. Just as important, you also want to make sure that you are representing different groups, so don't overlook leaders who may not have wide influence but who give voice to important sectors of your organization.

Selecting your CX Mission Statement team is a balancing act. You don't want to exclude anyone or any group that might later push back against a statement in which they were not involved—but if you try too hard to craft this statement by committee, the process can get very messy and protracted. That's when you end up with the Frankenstein version of a CX Mission Statement instead of something that can guide you and your organization forward. Keep it focused and concise.

Sometimes the best way to achieve this balance is with real events and timelines. We often run a series of workshops to get to the CX Mission Statement. The workshops include "homework" and voting on word choices. This type of collaboration with boundaries can help you get things done instead of wasting away in "we're not quite there" land.

Let's Talk About Values

Values, which are often not formally documented, need to be woven into the CX Mission Statement. If you have a list of more than three core values, you may not need to represent all of them in your CX Mission Statement. Instead, consider what is most important to your customers and the promises you made them. For example, while "providing quality products" might be part of your documented vision and values, I'd argue that it doesn't need to be said in your CX Mission Statement. Customers expect quality products; otherwise, they wouldn't be customers! Your CX

Mission Statement is unique to your organization...that's why you're doing all this digging.

Today, values are front and center for both customers and employees. Generations Z and now Alpha are making decisions based on aligned values. This guides where they shop, what brands they promote, and where they want to work. Their attitude is "I want to make sure my values align with who I do business with, who I work for, who I partner with, and how I invest my time and money."

If the people in your organization are not aligned around the organizational and personal values within your CX Mission Statement, then you're creating misalignment from the beginning. This misalignment causes anxiety for both customers and employees. Take, for example, the "quiet quitting" that was a hot topic of conversation in the years following the 2020 pandemic. Without much fanfare, employees are leaving their jobs because their organizations are not living up to the ideals and values that they espouse. When the actions of organizations don't reflect who they say they are, there are consequences internally and externally. Your goal is to create a CX Mission Statement as a beacon for your organization and a guide for your employees, an affirmation that the organization is living up to its values.

Bias Toward Action

Finally, don't let other initiatives delay your work on the CX Mission Statement.

Organizations are not stagnant entities. They are constantly moving, they are constantly evolving, and you might find yourself in a situation where the organization is already working on customer-facing innovations. Perhaps your organization is in the middle of a big branding project, or the organization has an initiative focusing on revamping its vision and values. That's great. That's important work. But don't look at those initiatives as reasons to stop working on the CX Mission Statement. Some of those projects could take months or even years. If you wait, you're missing an opportunity to start a culture shift in your organization around customer experience.

That's why it's important to have a *bias toward action*. Customer experience is often discussed without driving an organization's action. *Your* job as a CX Change Agent, should you choose to accept it, is to look for ways to act. This will drive the outcomes you ultimately want to achieve, even in nascent and imminent initiatives. If you have to adjust later based on the outcomes of those initiatives, so be it. Better to advance and adjust than to wait and do nothing.

STEP TWO: REFLECT

This is where we get thoughtful! It's time to reflect on four key questions that will become the four foundations of the statement.

CHAPTER 1

What's Our Brand Promise?

The first question is, What's our brand promise? What is the promise that we've made to our customers?

I often ask my audiences if they can recall feeling aligned with a brand promise. I typically use some examples many of us are familiar with.

Nike is known for its "Just Do It" campaigns. But its brand promise is actually to bring inspiration and innovation to every athlete in the world, with the understanding that if you have a body, you are an athlete. This is a great example of a brand promise that aligns the products it offers with the way its customers feel. I also like REI. REI's brand promise is to connect everyone to the outdoors.

Everything can be built from these ideas. When a brand promise is done well, you feel it.

Some organizations really struggle with their brand. Many misunderstand the brand promise with what they think shareholders want to hear. I won't shame anyone here, but trust me, your brand promise probably shouldn't include phrases like "best in class" or "deliver shareholder value."

To be clear, a brand promise is not always documented in writing. It's great when it is. Often, however, it needs to be gleaned from different written sources, as we discussed in the previous section on collecting. You might look at your marketing materials, for example, or at your public-facing communications to identify the themes that seem to bubble up repeatedly.

And don't forget to *ask*. Most people within an organization will have an idea about the organization's brand promise. If you have trouble answering this question yourself, informally poll a handful of people in the organization with whom you work closely. They might be from marketing, or market research, or a customer insights team. Engage with these people in rich discussions around questions like, *Who are we to our customers? What are they looking for? What is the promise that we are making?*

When reviewing their responses, look for consensus. Are you seeing common ground from people throughout your organization? If the responses are all over the map, you might have even more work to do than you realize. In that case, you might need to take a step back and convene a cross-functional group to address the question.

Explicit vs. Implicit Promises

You want to look for promises that are explicit in the documentation you gathered as well as promises that are implicit based on the relationships you want to develop with your customers. Some people may offer very specific answers when asked about the brand promise: "We're going to deliver our whatsits in the best possible way. We offer two-day shipping, which nobody else does." In all likelihood, this is not an explicit promise made to customers: "You will receive your order in two days because we're the fastest out there." Instead, this is probably more

CHAPTER 1

of an *implicit* promise that reflects your desire to serve the customer well. Either way, it is an important part of your brand promise.

There is often not a single, overarching brand promise articulated by the organization. This is when implicit promises—especially the many small, specific promises your organization makes to customers—offer clues to the organization's brand promise.

Don't Focus on the What

One important thing to remember when reflecting on your brand promise is to avoid focusing on the *what*. In leveraging your brand promise, you don't want to use product-specific language. Being the best whatsit maker in Whatsit Maker Land doesn't get to the heart of your brand promise. Think about the evolution of a company. A company usually starts with a product and then expands to offer other products. The company may also expand its services. Sometimes the company will make a complete pivot to a new set of products and services. And yet, throughout all this, they are still the same organization. The *whats*—product, product categories, services—do not change the core promise to customers that they want to keep.

When you get too focused on the *what*, you miss opportunities to really focus on the *why* and the *who*. So if you see product language sneaking into your CX Mission Statement, make the case that such language should not be included.

What's in It for the Customer?
The second question, which seems obvious but is easy to skip, is, What's in it for the customer?

In answering this question, you might again focus on descriptions of your products and services, even including sales performance: "We are the top-selling whatsit makers in America." That's wonderful for you...but how does it help the customer? What are your customers going to do with the whatsits that will help them lead a better life or be more well respected at work or accomplish whatever they want to accomplish? In short, what's actually in it for them?

Customers don't go to an REI store to buy a tent. They go there to get the right supplies so that they can have an adventure outside, so that they can feel venturesome and accomplished, or so that they can make a connection to nature. That is what's in it for REI customers. It's not about the products or services—it's about what your customers can achieve, feel, and do with those products and services.

As with the first question ("What's our brand promise?"), answering "What's in it for the customer?" is a great opportunity to brainstorm—through rich conversations and discussions—with other people in your organization. You might be surprised by their answers, what they focus on, or what they believe is being delivered compared to what is actually happening.

CHAPTER 1

Let's say that you work in a bank. If you ask, "What's in it for the customer?" you might get a reply such as, "A safe place to keep their money." That's true, but that's what every bank does. That is literally the definition of a bank. In fact, saving their money in a safe place isn't the outcome that customers are seeking. They want to *do* something. They want to live their life a certain way. They want to save to have a house. They want to make sure their money is earning on their behalf. They want to make sure that they have access to funds when they need them for their daily lives. Start thinking about what your customers are really trying to do and why you are different and better positioned than other organizations or companies to help them do it. Why, in sum, would somebody pick your bank over another bank?

It might be helpful to think beyond your industry. "They want to save their money in a safe place" isn't going to cut it. Think beyond the commoditized version of who you are. And do not assume that customers understand why you're special—especially if you tout attributes shared with every other bank!

Focus on who you are and the promise that makes you special. Look at the innovations in your organization, for these often emerge from a desire to help people get to their goals faster. You may need to look into your institutional history; sometimes a sea change from thirty years ago—something everyone now takes for granted—is the key to unlocking your organization's promise to help the customer reach their goals.

That's what you want to focus on: the goals of the customer. Because here's one of the hard truths about customer experience work: *Customers do not think about your brand.* They do not wake up and think, *I cannot wait to go to the bank.* Instead, they think about their goals and desires, how they want to feel, how they want to live. The question of what's in it for the customer can never be far from your mind if you want to craft a powerful *Customer* Experience Mission Statement.

What Can We Consistently Deliver?
Consistency is one of the most important characteristics of meaningful customer experience. You have to be consistent in what you deliver. This can be tricky, because it's human nature to want to promise the best, promise the most, promise the fastest. But your CX Mission Statement has to be based on the experience that you can always deliver, no matter what.

Begin by avoiding superlatives, those words that end in *-est* that are nearly impossible to deliver consistently: the fastest, the greatest, the easiest, the best. It's hard to consistently deliver on superlatives. There are situations when you are going to miss something. Humans make mistakes, machines make mistakes, and customer expectations change. So be honest about what you can accomplish. You won't be the best all the time. You won't be the fastest all the time. And the danger is that the minute you've made that promise, somebody doesn't deliver on that promise; then you are not delivering on your mission.

Perhaps you already have an *-est* expectation in your mission. What should you do with it? The answer is to think about what you're truly trying to say. Be very clear about what that *-est* means for the customer and what it means for your behavior as well. You want to be the fastest. Great. What does that really mean? It might mean you want to be responsive, and you want to deliver in the most expedited way you can. Don't stop there. Dig deeper. To be the fastest, you need to be responsive to your customers, but what does that look like? How long does it take before it's a problem? What standards are you setting to ensure you meet this mission requirement?

And—lest we take our eye off the ball—what about being fast is great for customers? Is it to help them achieve their goals faster and easier? Can we integrate those goals into our promise? Now that's a great CX mission!

I hope you're starting to see why crafting the CX Mission Statement carefully is so important: It will influence and put pressure on you, your organization's behavior and decisions, and even your corporate culture.

Start with Single Words

One suggestion as you brainstorm around the question of what you can consistently deliver is to start with single words, such as *friendly* or *value*. Can you consistently, without exception, deliver friendly service? Can you consistently, without exception, deliver value? Again, avoid the superlatives. We want to balance the aspirational with the attainable. Don't aim to deliver the *best* value. Promise only that the customer will always get value from their interactions with your company. You can stand by that, and the customer will (perhaps subconsciously) appreciate your discipline in avoiding the superlative. Nobody believes the gas station on the corner sells "the coldest beer in town."

Some other words to think about: Can you always be *authentic*? Can you always be *honest*? Can you always be *transparent*? Don't answer too hastily. Consistency is harder than you might think. For example, some of you are in industries where you can't be transparent all the time. So be realistic. What can you train and empower your people to do consistently? It's okay to be aspirational about these ideas when you are clear about your values. Maybe you aren't as transparent as you'd like to be *yet*—but you are on your way. The CX Mission Statement will be there to serve those aspirations so that the entire organization can align around these ideals.

This question, "What experience can we consistently deliver?," gets to the heart of who you are and how you want to show up throughout the customer journey—no matter who the customer is, no matter what product they're buying, and no matter where they are in the journey. Answering this question and including the answers in the CX Mission Statement also gives you the right language and tools to evaluate when things go wrong. If you say you are going to provide value in a certain way, and then you don't, you can evaluate what went wrong with your employees. You can say, for example, "We said that in everything we do, we're going to provide a certain value. Why didn't it happen this time?"

Having said all this, I don't want you to be afraid to be aspirational. For example, maybe you want to deliver friendly service no matter what as part of your brand promise. You look around and think, *Oh, we're not there yet.* That's okay. If that's where you want to go, if you want that to be part of your promise to your customer, you can include "friendly service, no matter what" in your CX Mission Statement. Why? Because, unlike being the best or being the fastest, this is something you can achieve. (Bonus thoughts: Consider also what the word *friendly* means at your organization. What are standards that would align with that as part of your mission?)

Be Realistic

I can't tell you how many CX Mission Statements I've seen that start off as completely unrealistic wishes instead of real-world guides. There are realities we can't avoid. You might be in a regulated industry or in a fast-paced, highly competitive one. It might not be realistic to claim to be innovating in a regulated industry or to be calm and reassuring in a highly competitive environment.

One example I saw of this unrealistic approach was in a company that served travelers. They wanted to deliver exceptional service to every customer, every time. Ahem... Have you traveled lately? The inevitable crowded airports, long lines at hotel registration desks, and technology glitches basically guarantee that your experience as a traveler is hardly going to be exceptional every time. It's not fair to ask your employees to do the impossible.

Being aspirational and ambitious is encouraged, but being realistic is what's most important. For example, there may be a moment when you feel that you haven't been delivering on the expectations of your clients and customers according to your promise. If you know, however, that you can get there, that's okay. You can still put that promise into the CX Mission Statement.

But if there's something that you've never been able to deliver on, something you're just putting out there on a hope and a prayer, that's not going to work, because people aren't going to buy into it inside the organization. The deliverable has to be close enough to reality that when your people hear it, they realize it's not totally aspirational—it's something they can deliver. If you find the sweet spot in the middle of aspirational and realistic, you'll get the buy-in and support to turn aspiration into reality.

The Humble Lawyers: A True Story

You might be surprised at what makes you special. We once worked with a law firm that *insisted* they were like every other law firm. They had professionals, they had expertise, and they were willing to go the extra mile for their clients ... just like every other law firm.

Then we started questioning some of their customers and people throughout the organization. (This is a great way to get real-world perspectives!)

What we heard wasn't about professional expertise—that was a given. What emerged again and again was how these lawyers showed up a bit differently than other lawyers: The clients felt they showed up with humility instead of arrogance. This was manifested by a willingness to listen first and then talk. Clients felt they were respected and felt an open-mindedness from the attorneys, the assistants, and everyone at the firm. This humility was a core characteristic of the founders of the firm. Being humble was who the founders were, and that humility was embedded into the culture of their firm. It was so embedded, in fact, that the lawyers didn't necessarily recognize it ... but it made a big difference to their clients. And the humility with which the lawyers showed up consistently put the firm in a slightly different category than every other law firm. That mission wrote itself.

What Do We Want Our Customers to Feel?
The final question is vital to providing the best customer experience: What do we want our customers to feel?

The goal here is to get at the heart of the emotions elicited by your organization through its products, services, and people. You're looking for a deeper response than, for example, wanting your customers to feel confident and satisfied. Imagine if someone asked how you felt about your relationship with a friend, and you responded, "Very satisfied." Hardly a ringing endorsement of that relationship. Likewise, with this question you want to seek deeper emotions.

To return to the REI example, their customers want to feel more adventurous, more connected to nature. Depending on your business, perhaps your goal is to make your customers feel secure or free or creative. The important thing is to find those one or two words that capture exactly how you want your organization to make your customers feel. Because in every single experience that customers have, they are trying to achieve a goal and are trying to feel something.

What do customers say about why they like working with you? Look for words that really showcase their emotions. You might see a pattern around feeling "relieved" or "happily surprised." Dig into that type of feedback to identify those all-important emotions that will serve as your guide to promises made and promises kept. Between what the customers want to feel and the specifics that make your organization unique, your customer experience mission should be starting to come together.

As with the previous questions, this is a good opportunity to brainstorm with different people in your organization—although I have found in my experience as a CX consultant that in many industries, people are not used to

CHAPTER 1

considering feelings or emotions linked to their work. Some might be scientists in the healthcare field or engineers or manufacturing specialists for whom talking about "how we want our customers to feel" might seem a bit foreign. They don't want to embrace those ideas, which can present a challenge to those of you trying to get this question answered. But humans are emotional creatures. We need to embrace this truth about our customers.

What About Negative Emotions?
Of course, identifying a positive emotion for your customers may not be as easy as it sounds. For example, let's say you are an insurance company handling claims. Your customers are likely to be upset or concerned when they arrive at your door. They may even be wary about what you can do for them. They might be disappointed with your response, perhaps expecting more than they were entitled to. In any case, the interactions with your customers are not occurring in a fun context. The fact is, as an insurance company, you are not going to be able to make your customers feel *happy* all the time. But what can you help them feel? You can help them feel *secure* that they're getting the right information, that they have the right plan, that they are covered when they need to be covered.

Look for Real-World Examples
It's also important to look to real-world examples for indications of how customers might feel. Customer

feedback will be extremely valuable here. Look for the words they use when they say they're feeling connected to your brand, when they're feeling really good. Or you can look at the negative feedback and think about the opposite of the feelings they are expressing. If customers are telling you they're feeling frustrated, for example, you know that you want them to feel cared for and relieved. If they say they're feeling angry, you want them to feel calm and grateful. Of course, many customers don't come right out and say, "I'm feeling _____." Pay attention to the words they are using, because many customers will communicate how they feel without saying, "This is how I feel."

Sometimes, CX professionals will go overboard in trying to identify the deep feelings of every unique customer persona. It's important to stay realistic. Don't forget that your customers are just living their real lives. I have seen a number of very excited people say, "We're going to get everybody to feel like they're treated exceptionally, that they are truly connected to our brand!" Those are wonderful aspirations, but you have to get real. What are they looking for? Do they just need to feel respected? Do they just need to feel efficient? Do they feel frustrated that they need to call in about an issue in the first place? Think carefully about what it is you want customers to feel in their real lives.

Finally, when all is said and done, you might come up with more words or adjectives than you will use in your

CHAPTER 1

Our CX Mission Statement... *fill in the blanks:*

At _____ our customers expect
Your organization's name

_____
1. Brand promise

in order to _____
2. What's in it for the customer

_____ .

We deliver that experience consistently by _____

_____
3. What experience can we consistently deliver

_____ so our customers feel

_____
4. What do we want our customers to feel

_____ along every step of

their journey.

Connect Template

CX Mission Statement. That's okay. Even if you don't use some of those words, just brainstorming that list will give you ideas about how to address customer experience, including where to improve the customer experience journey.

STEP THREE: CONNECT

Once you've answered these four questions, you are ready to put the results of your brainstorming into your CX Mission Statement using the template shown on the previous page.

Your final CX Mission Statement may not be constructed precisely along the lines of the template. I've seen many teams mix things up, resulting in a different construct for their statement. Nevertheless, these four questions—"What's our brand promise?" "What's in it for the customer?" "What can we consistently deliver?" and "What do we want our customers to feel?"—capture the four key elements that must be included in your CX Mission Statement. The objective is to avoid a "statement" that includes multiple paragraphs with seventeen bullet points. The CX Mission Statement is something you want people to internalize. Remember that you are shaping their mindset about the organization and its customers. People need to hear or see the CX Mission Statement and think, *Okay, I get it*. And when you ask them a week later to describe it, they should be able to get close.

Remember the messy first draft of your collection notes? Even in the first draft of the full-fledged statement, the filled-in template is often long and overstuffed. Take that first draft and start narrowing down what you include. Ask yourself, *Do we really need to say that? Can we separate this? Can we move this here?* It's also a good exercise to ask if you're repeating yourself redundantly. ☺ Do you need to say "safe

CHAPTER 1

and secure"? Pick the most important attribute that makes your organization ... well ... your organization.

Your CX Mission Statement is meant to be internalized. I'd recommend no more than four lines—fewer if you can manage it.

Let's talk about a few examples. Like most statements, you may think some of these are less than perfect. But having an imperfect CX mission defined is better than not having one at all! It's not meant to solve all your problems; it's a reminder of who you are and what customers can expect.

This one is for a utility company. They had the unique circumstance of delivering their best experiences when nothing happened. They didn't want their customers to think about them at all!

> "Our customers expect reliability so they can live and work with ease and confidence. By proactively meeting their needs, our customers feel valued along every step of their journey."

This worked for them because it was a reminder that reliability was about helping customers live their lives. That sentiment coincided with a culture shift toward proactively addressing needs instead of reacting to service issues. The statement took many drafts and versions, but once it was completed, the company rolled it out to every team and began using it on a regular basis.

Another interesting example comes from a manufacturing organization. I've redacted the type of products they made here, but they were often used to make other machines work—important machines like MRIs and rockets.

> "We **go beyond** our innovative products, delivering the **dependability** you need to **succeed**."

Their products were definitely innovative, but they knew they would be copied and commoditized eventually. We identified that a differentiator for them was their success with installation and cooperation with their customers. We also leaned into the "go beyond" idea to help remind everyone what these customers were doing with the products.

Finding your statement won't be easy, not least because you, your CX team, and the other non-CX team members involved will all contribute wonderful ideas and perspectives on the questions at hand. You will need to consolidate those ideas and perspectives to find the right words.

Sorting the Ideas

A good way to consolidate the elements of the first draft is to have people vote to rank the ideas. There might be, for example, three responses to the question of how you consistently show up for your customers. Ask your team to rank those three answers and see if one takes precedence over the others. Then you can perhaps bring in unique elements of the other two ideas to finish with a consolidated but concise answer.

It's also important to prioritize ideas. You may want to be *valuable* and want to be *fun* and want to be *friendly* and want to be *secure*—all those things to all the customers. But you need to prioritize who you are and what makes you different. Be judicious about words that reflect your industry but don't differentiate your organization from any other (such as the example of working in a bank). And avoid vague generalizations. Have somebody read the CX Mission Statement draft aloud, and ask yourself, *How do I know it's talking about us?* If the statement is too vague, it will feel like every other organization in your industry. Again, make sure that you are truly identifying who you are for *your* customers.

Word Battles

Battles among team members about which specific words to use can become intense. You might find the team going back and forth about whether to say *sustainable* or *scalable* until somebody says, "Just put them both in there!" That might be a solution, but you want to be careful with each word you decide to include in the statement. Sometimes, as a team, you just need to pick the top word—or the top three words that you want to use if you cannot reach a consensus on a single word.

Passionate discussions about the nuances of a word or words can take up quite a bit of time. Sometimes, as the leader or facilitator, you have to take control and say, "Okay, I'm hearing this group is saying this is important, while that group is saying that is important. Let's go ahead and either come up with a new word or just vote right now. Which word is better?"

Also, remind your team that perfect is the enemy of good. In other words, if you try too hard to make it perfect, you will never finish. Just decide if a word is good enough; if it is, it's time for the team to move on.

People get very invested in this process, and that's a good thing. But at the end of the day, you want a tool that you can use to internalize the mindset at the core of your mission. If there are too many words, that is too hard to do. Avoid the trap of trying to put in all the different words and getting into debates about nuances when really you just need to say, "We want to be responsive."

Watch Your Language

Perhaps the most important lesson to keep in mind concerning individual words is to avoid corporate or industry speak at all times. This might be more difficult than you imagine; corporate speak can become so prevalent you might not even realize you're using it. As the saying goes, it's hard to read the label of the jar you're in. Since everyone around you in the organization understands the language you're using, you might forget that the language is, in fact, specific to your industry or your organization or perhaps even to your team or business unit. Here's a simple way to test whether you are using corporate or industry speak: Are there words

CHAPTER 1

in the CX Mission Statement that you use in your industry but that you might not use when talking to a friend? If so, put up a little red flag and rethink those words.

It's also important to keep products and specific acronyms out of the mindset statement. I have often seen leaders who want to use their CX Mission Statement to brag about a specific advancement of their company—a new technology, a cleverly branded tool, or the like. This is short-term thinking. Your CX mindset should be set up for success well beyond the next few products you roll out or the recent rebranding. Your CX mindset is about who you are to your customers, not the products you sell. What your customers do with your products to improve their lives is far more important.

After all, you want your CX Mission Statement to be something people feel and internalize, which is not easy to do with a statement filled with industry language, acronyms, or corporate speak. Think of the CX Mission Statement examples I spoke of earlier. One of them talked about living and working with ease and confidence, and one of them talked about going beyond. That's not corporate speak. This is your goal in crafting the CX Mission Statement: to use phrases that are meaningful enough to describe your organization's mindset about your customers without specific references to your products, services, or anything else around how your organization is structured.

The Boss Suggests...
Sometimes, as a CX team, you are crafting a concise and memorable statement only to find your leadership keeps adding to it. This is something I've encountered quite a bit. Those leaders might be missing the point, trying to keep the statement focused on the products, or all the values of the company, or recent fiscal achievements. That's where voting can be very powerful. Ask different groups to rank and prioritize ideas.

Of course, sometimes there are battles that you cannot win. All is not lost, however, because great statements become a kind of shorthand. For example, let's say you have a three-paragraph CX Mission Statement because the writing process went horribly awry: Your leaders or other teams kept adding to it, and now it's just too long!

Look for what you can feature from the statement as a kind of shorthand. Look for the phrases that you know are really going to push people forward the most. The utility company we discussed did a great job at formulating a concise CX Mission Statement. However, in the beginning there was some pushback to keeping it concise, and the statement just kept getting longer. One group wanted to emphasize the expertise of their repair team. One group felt it was important to say customers were valued and appreciated. So we started saying the key phrases that mattered to them.

"What's the real goal of sharing the expertise?" I'd ask.

"So customers can feel confident."

"Good. You want customers to feel *confident*. Let's work with that."

As you continue to build the statement, use those key phrases again and again. A lot of times, people are saying the same thing in different ways.

You can do this for your mission, too, because the more you use it as shorthand, the more people start recognizing it as the true mission they are internalizing. Look for ways to extrapolate the most important elements of the statement and use those elements as shorthand.

For example, you could repeatedly use the valuable shorthand phrase you identified, always including "from our CX Mission Statement" in your citation. With this approach, you're not saying the key phrase is the whole thing, but you're reminding people of the ideals, emotions, and other key elements while leaving out the less important additions. We did this with the manufacturing organization as well, reminding everyone to "go beyond" and to help the customers *feel* that the company was going beyond.

Another approach to keeping the CX Mission Statement concise is to ask "why" again and again. If someone is trying to push something into the statement that seems extraneous to you, it's fair to ask them, "Why would we want this in there?"

And they might say, "Well, those are our products."

Ask them, "Why is that important for our mission?"

Their response might be, "Because that's what we do."

Don't give up! Keep asking. "Why is that relevant to our customers' emotions and how we show up for them?" Clearly, this line of questioning can become a bit uncomfortable. I recognize that you have to be aware of the culture of your organization (that is, how much you can push back). But if you can keep asking the questions, sometimes you can find a persuasive argument. For example, you might get them to a place where you could say, "This is already in our service offer, so we don't really need it in our CX Mission Statement."

Another great question is, "What happens when a customer uses that product?" This allows you to explore how those products aren't really what the customer wants. They want what the product or service helps them do, achieve, and feel. That's CX gold.

The bottom line: You want a statement that is short, memorable, engaging, and useful. Note that short and memorable often go together. When you start adding, your text starts losing its power. A long text is more difficult to internalize. I have lost this battle with some of my clients. I have seen their statements get bloated. They will never be as effective as something that people can point to and say, "Yes, that's our mission. I get it. I'm tucking it into my heart. I'll use it to guide everything I do."

CHAPTER 2

CREATE THE MINDSET—USING YOUR CX MISSION STATEMENT

It's time to fight the fluff.

I'll bet you've heard your colleagues discuss customer experience as if it's about "soft skills"; they may even use vague terms like *fluffy*. It's easy to assume a strong CX Mission Statement is more of that "soft" stuff. It's important to meet this challenge head-on and show how you'll use the statement not just as a poster on the wall but as a tool for measuring how you're doing, for recognizing and rewarding employees, and perhaps most importantly, for making sure you're living up to the true mission behind your promise to customers.

Shifting a mindset is no small task. The CX Mission Statement is key.

"What good can a statement do?" I've been asked.

The answer is *a lot*. But it works only if you work it.

The CX Mission Statement is intended to be a tool. The goal is not to create another document that lies around the office unread and unused. It is not something you file away where people have to go find it. Nor is it something you just frame and put on the wall. This is a tool that helps people understand and internalize the organization's mindset toward its customers. It is a tool for action and change—a tool that, if well written, you can use every day.

Let's define what it can be used for:

1. It's a reminder to everyone of what promises have been made, what aspirational experience you want to deliver, and what your products and services actually do for your customers' lives.
2. It's a gut-check measurement that creates a universal language. Did we live up to this? Why or why not? What can we do next time?
3. It's a recognition tool to share when employees and teams live up to that mission—or don't.

Think about the places in your workflow where you will use the CX Mission Statement. When you're writing the role descriptions for the next person on your team, you will use the CX Mission Statement. When you're thinking about which priority you're going to focus on next, you will use the CX Mission Statement. Setting goals, coaching, or leading your team are more opportunities to use the CX Mission Statement.

CHAPTER 2

Any statement—mission statement, vision statement, purpose statement—is aspirational. It's the goal. Crafting a CX Mission Statement is important because it gives you and your organization the target to strive for. The challenge is how to achieve that target. How do you take this tool and use it to guide your behaviors and decisions? To be more specific: How will you use the CX Mission Statement to direct the way you create new products, services, processes, and initiatives?

This is not a question to be answered once. It's a question that must be answered continuously, whenever a decision about your organization's products, services, processes, and initiatives is required.

Living CX: Putting Your CX Mission Statement to Work

Hang on, because we are about to detail how a CX Mission Statement can be used to create cultural change, keep the customer top of mind, hire and onboard employees, develop products or services, improve sales or marketing, measure success, improve employee training and performance, improve communication, and align your organization's vision and goals. Whew!

Use this list of ideas to inspire your own creativity. Each culture is unique, so lean into what makes yours special.

Creating Cultural Change

The challenge here is to shift your culture to become a customer-centric organization. This is all about creating a mindset that aligns everyone in the organization. It takes more than talk. The CX Mission Statement is the tool to help you facilitate the first step of a culture shift toward customer-centricity. That first step is defining who you are trying to be to your customers; the next step is getting everyone on board with the defined mission. This is where, no matter where you are in the organization, partnering with your internal communications team is incredibly helpful—as is partnering with different parts of your C-suite. So think carefully about how you are presenting the mission and engaging with people throughout the organization.

Here are some ideas to create cultural change:

- Discuss the CX Mission Statement during leadership meetings: Ensure executives and managers lead by example in upholding the mission.
- Incorporate the CX Mission Statement into team-building exercises: Use it as a basis for shared goals and collaboration.
- Use the CX Mission Statement to inspire innovation: Encourage employees to generate ideas that align with the company's purpose.

Keeping the Customer Top of Mind

As we talk about keeping customers top of mind, it's important to remember that the CX Mission Statement is not something you would necessarily share with your customers—because it is not intended for customers. It is, instead, an internal document that you use to make sure everybody is consistently showing up for customers in the same way.

After all, the definition of *customer-centricity* is putting the customer at the center of all you do. To do that well, you need a well-defined CX mission. Here are some tips for using the CX Mission Statement to keep the customer top of mind:

- Use the CX Mission Statement as a reference point for resolving customer issues: Ensure that resolutions align with the desired experience.
- Use the CX Mission Statement as a framework for handling customer complaints: Address issues while keeping the desired experience in mind.
- Use the CX Mission Statement to inform service recovery strategies: Turn negative experiences into positive ones aligned with the desired customer experience.

Hiring and Onboarding Employees

You want to incorporate your CX mission in the process of hiring and onboarding employees. This is one of my favorite uses of the CX Mission Statement because you will attract the people who say, "Yeah, I want to live that mission." Here are specific tips for using the CX Mission Statement as part of your hiring and onboarding process:

- Refer to the CX Mission Statement in job descriptions: Help potential candidates understand the company's values and goals.
- Share the CX Mission Statement during onboarding: Introduce new employees to the company's purpose and values from day one.

- Include the CX Mission Statement in employee handbooks: Reinforce the CX Mission Statement as a guiding principle for all employees.

Developing Products or Services

You can use the CX Mission Statement to test new product or service ideas. For example, someone might say, "We need to develop a totally new whatsit." You might think about it and ask, "How will that help customers experience our mission?" A discussion around the CX mission can help you prioritize so that you put effort and investment in the places that consistently deliver on customer experience. Here's how to use the CX mission to help guide your product or service development:

- Use the CX Mission Statement as a foundation for creating customer personas: Understand customers' needs and tailor experiences accordingly.
- Use the CX Mission Statement to inform product or service development: Ensure that offerings address customers' pain points and expectations.
- Create a customer journey map aligned with the CX Mission Statement: Visualize the desired experience and identify areas for improvement.

Improving Sales and Marketing

The CX Mission Statement is naturally vital in setting sales and marketing priorities. After all, the CX mission is at the core of the promise you make to customers—a promise that happens early in the customer journey in marketing and sales. Even if you don't share the actual mission statement, incorporating the ideas and values behind it can help build the customer journey authentically from the beginning. Communicating with sales and marketing as you develop the CX Mission Statement and including representatives from sales and marketing in the development process is key. Here are ideas for ensuring that the CX Mission Statement is at the core of your sales and marketing efforts:

- Share customer success stories that align with the CX Mission Statement: Highlight examples of exceptional (and not-so-great) experiences; sales often makes promises and doesn't know when they aren't being realized with customers.
- Incorporate the CX Mission Statement into social media strategies: Engage with customers in ways that align with the desired experience.
- Create visuals or infographics representing the CX Mission Statement: Make it visually appealing and easy to remember.

Measuring Success

Another important role for the CX Mission Statement is to help you define what needs to be measured. As we will see later in this book, the other two pillars of customer experience—the CX Success Blueprint and the CX Charter—rely on the CX Mission Statement. Therefore, you want to make sure that when you are defining success going forward, the Mission Statement is your North Star. That means you should:

- Develop key performance indicators (KPIs) that align with the CX Mission Statement: Measure success based on delivering the desired experiences. (We'll be diving into the many facets of delivering CX success in the next part of the book.)
- Include the CX Mission Statement in employee feedback surveys: Gather feedback on how well the organization is delivering on its customer experience goals.
- Ask employees if they feel the experience is aligned in how employees deliver for one another too. Success means solid alignment around mindset and behaviors, inside and outside the organization.

Improving Employee Training and Performance

We've talked about the importance of buy-in throughout the organization as one of the key factors for the successful adoption of a CX Mission Statement. Of equal importance is know-how, especially at the employee level. The guidelines offered by the CX Mission Statement can help improve the training of employees and their subsequent performance. This list includes key steps that can improve training programs and enhance employee performance:

- Host a mission moments workshop: Ask employees to identify when the team delivered and when they

didn't. Break down the why behind both and create processes and best practices for long-term success.
- Incorporate the CX Mission Statement into customer service training programs: Your frontline employees need to feel connected to how their interactions align with the defined customer experience.
- Celebrate employees who embody the CX Mission Statement: Recognize and reward those who consistently deliver outstanding service.

Improving Communication

Simply put, you can't discuss your CX mission enough!

You never want to stop communicating and training on your CX mission. It used to be said that people need to hear something seven times in different ways to remember it. That number is going up. Our attention spans are shorter. We have too many points of input. We consume so much more content than we used to. Now we have to put the CX Mission Statement in front of people again and again and again and again and again, forever. Because if we stop repeating it, if we stop communicating about it, people will start ignoring it, believing it's one of those documents made to be filed and forgotten—or engraved on a wall for your people to walk by every day without ever thinking about how it impacts their work. Here are some suggestions for making sure your people are thinking about and using the CX Mission Statement every day.

- Create internal campaigns that revolve around the CX Mission Statement: Generate enthusiasm and reinforce its importance.
- Encourage employees to share personal stories related to the customer experience mission: Foster an emotional connection to the purpose.
- Incorporate the CX Mission Statement into annual reports and investor presentations: Demonstrate the company's commitment to serving its customers.

Aligning Organizational Vision and Goals

Finally, the CX Mission Statement must align the organization's goals in all organizational activities with its overall vision. Here are a few ways to ensure the CX Mission Statement fulfills this function:

- Use the CX Mission Statement to guide decision-making at all levels of the organization: Ensure choices align with the desired customer experience.
- Use the CX Mission Statement to identify opportunities for process improvements: Streamline operations to better support the desired customer experience.
- Use the CX Mission Statement to guide product or service development: Ensure that offerings align with the company's purpose.

This list, although not exhaustive, is a good starting point for the on-the-ground implementation of your CX

CHAPTER 2

Mission Statement—it will lead to unforgettable mission moments for your customers.

Begin by highlighting the items that are most relevant to your organization. What could you do tomorrow? What could you do in a year? What could you do in two years? Start to build momentum and never let up. A CX Mission Statement is not something that you just release, and then everybody says, "Oh, I get it! This is great! We've got a CX Mission Statement! Boom, we are customer-centric!" Unfortunately, that's not how it works. You have to start introducing and communicating and repeating and using and socializing and celebrating and creating a pattern of use so that people know this isn't a flavor of the month, this isn't something you're just talking about. This is something you're using in your organization to deliver on the promises that you've made and to be consistently who you are to your customers throughout their journey.

Final Thoughts on Your CX Mission Statement

I'm a big believer in creating, using, and internalizing a CX Mission Statement. That's because I know it's a crucial element in success.

The goal of the CX Mission Statement is to create a universal language around the idea of an experience mindset. We want to inspire the right decisions and actions throughout the organization. If you find that your statement has lost its way, that it's too long, that it's not really delivering in the way that you want ... you are allowed to evolve and make every effort to change. You might, for example, bring a different cross-functional group together and say, "Let's work together to develop a CX Mission Statement that is specific to who we are and how we deliver."

Remember, don't focus on products or on transactions—focus on *who* is engaged in the customer experience mission. You want to make sure that you are showing up in the most positive and proactive way for your customers and that you are delivering not only on behalf of who *they* are but also on behalf of who *you* are. And that's where you get that magic alignment. That's where you start getting people to understand this is the North Star, this is something you can tuck into your hearts. The CX mission is something you internalize and turn into behaviors and actions. And that's what this is all about.

CHAPTER 3

CUSTOMER EXPERIENCE IS A STRATEGY— DEFINING YOUR CX SUCCESS BLUEPRINT

THE DEFINITION OF STRATEGY IS "AN INTENTIONALLY DEVELoped plan or method for achieving a goal."

When I say that customer experience is a strategy, I mean that customer experience is based on a plan that is designed to reach specific goals. You have to define your goals so that you can take the right steps to achieve those goals.

In customer experience, we often skip this part! Many customer experience teams don't have real goals. (Sorry, not sorry if this is the case where you are.)

Some customer experience "goals" are actually measurements. Many CX teams have goals such as "improve our NPS score" or "achieve higher survey response rates." These are tactics; they are not strategies. The organization wants to achieve higher response rates without knowing how those higher response rates will help the organization succeed. This is where we have to get real and honest about what CX can and can't do: We can't force customers to take surveys, and it doesn't really matter if they do. Those surveys and NPS ratings give us information to use, yes, but they aren't actual outcomes that our C-suite will see and think, *Yes! That's success.*

In other organizations I have worked with, the CX teams and executives describe broad, feel-good goals such as "be the best" or "deliver a great experience to every customer." At the end of the year, they discover they aren't quite sure if they were successful.

Your goals may sound reasonable and relevant—but take a closer look. For example, "We want to be very good at serving customers quickly and accurately" might sound like a reasonable customer experience goal. But there are two problems. First, it is rather vague. How do you know when you are "being very good at serving customers quickly and accurately"? Second, how does "being very good at serving customers" help your organization? Let's say as a retailer, you decide being open twenty-four hours a day would help customers. Given the costs in payroll and overhead of such hours, does this goal help your organization achieve its goals?

Specific, achievable customer experience goals define success. And that customer experience success counts only if the CX goals are aligned with the goals of your organization and its leaders. That's why it's up to us, the CX leaders, to understand and articulate how our efforts will drive the results and outcomes our C-suite is looking for. Higher revenue. Lower expenses.

CHAPTER 3

Unfortunately, customer experience is not viewed the same way as other parts of the organization. Can you imagine a world where the sales team was given the task of "selling lots of things to every customer"? Of course not! Sales has clear goals and expected outcomes, so they adjust their efforts and plans to achieve those outcomes. Sometimes that means selling more products to current customers. Sometimes that means finding more customers to sell to. Sometimes that means achieving more operational efficiency to keep costs down. Each of these connects to overall organizational health. And there are real numbers attached to these goals.

To define your CX strategy in ways that ensure your customer experience goals are aligned with your organizational goals, flip your thinking and start with what your organization and leaders need, *then* build your CX goals around those outcomes.

This is the piece I see missing in most customer experience programs—and even in some of the big-name books and customer service theories. Customer experience is often approached as a bunch of discrete things you just *do*. And the defined outcomes are often things a CX leader can't possibly achieve on their own. For example, improving net promoter score (NPS) or other customer feedback scores is fine, but it requires cross-functional thinking and leadership to translate those improved scores into improvement of the actual customer experience. Simply measuring and reporting NPS, as many CX leaders are asked to do, is not enough to change the customer experience. It is unfair to put CX leaders in that position.

When your leaders are not thinking strategically about CX, you have to put forward a clearly defined strategy that links your CX activities to the organization's goals. If you're getting worried about ruffling feathers, relax. The next set of guidelines will help you go about your task while getting buy-in from the C-suite and beyond.

Four Questions for an Effective Strategy

To develop an effective customer experience strategy, you can ask yourself these questions:

1. **What specific outcomes will be most meaningful?** You can almost apply any outcome to customer experience, so if you're not careful, you could have a list of a hundred things. The employee experience relates to customer experience, for example. One could say the disruption of the supply chain also impacts customer experience. The list is endless. So you have to become adept at discerning which outcomes will be the most meaningful.
2. **How do these outcomes align with your organizational goals?** The more you prioritize outcomes that align with your organizational goals, the more everyone wins.
3. **What metrics should be measured to ensure you are achieving the outcomes?** They might not be the ones you expect.

4. **What are the realistic parameters with which you'll define success?** Customer experience leaders often have big goals they have not broken down. They will say things like, "Well, our goal is to increase market share, and we are going to do that by having the most amazing customer experience. Our NPS will go up, and that will drive more people to the business, and it will grow." That sounds great, but it's back to the magical thinking I wrote about in part 1. You have to break down your success into specific parameters:

- What kind of tools do we need?
- What resources do we have?
- Do we have the buy-in we need?

Four Considerations in Developing a Strategic Plan

First, *look at big picture goals.* You may have explicitly outlined organizational goals. (Kudos if you do, because many organizations don't.) However, there are often unwritten goals that everyone still knows about.

One common example is a goal with which the CEO is obsessed. Let's say every time your CEO gets onstage or has a town hall or shares information, she will say something about needing to beat a competitor. It never fails. "We need to beat Company B. We must beat Company B." That's all she cares about.

But what is she really talking about? Well, she might be talking about gaining more market share. So the big picture goal in this example is gaining market share.

Sometimes, looking at the big picture goals can be overwhelming. Some organizations will have big goals around sustainability or around safety or around any number of very broad areas. As a customer experience leader, your job is to zero in on where you can have an impact—an area that other people in your organization will consider worthwhile and meaningful. Sustainability is a major focus for many organizations right now. Customer experience and sustainability can go hand in hand. If sustainability is what everyone is talking about, if sustainability is what your shareholders are talking about, if it's what your leaders are talking about, then start there.

Second, *consider broader leadership goals.* It's especially important to consider the goals of all your C-suite leaders—not just the CEO. What does your chief financial officer care about? What does your chief marketing officer care about? Sometimes the chief revenue officer or the chief product officer will have a lot of sway in the C-suite. What are their primary concerns? What's topmost in their minds? Every organization is going to be a little different here, so you need to be an investigator.

You need to figure out what is going on with each person who has the influence that you depend on. This is key to ensure that the top leaders in your organization understand what you are doing and why it is valuable. I've witnessed layoffs and CX teams being cut down because they did not make their case to the C-suite. Your chief financial officer needs to hear why investing in CX is meaningful to your overall financial success. Your chief operating officer wants to hear about how investing in CX will help everyone do their job more efficiently. You get the idea.

Third, you need to *convey specific outcomes and metrics*. Don't simply declare that you will be improving a customer feedback score, for example. First, as we mentioned, NPS is just a measurement; it is not actually something that will drive the business forward until you can make the case that it will. So be specific. Explain why you're collecting this feedback, why you're tracking these metrics, and what you believe these metrics will do. If you intend to increase a specific score, explain what that means to the organization. For example, you could say it means the organization has happier customers who will stay longer, which will drive your revenue with higher customer lifetime value and more word-of-mouth referrals, which will lead to X, Y, and Z. Perhaps the outcome in your sights is higher market share because you know market share is what the CEO and CFO are paying attention to. This is your opportunity to connect the dots with a more enhanced and robust customer referral program.

In sum, we're talking about layers. You have to think about a customer experience strategy as what the organization really cares about, what your leaders really care about, and where your efforts will make the most sense. Sometimes you spend all your efforts collecting data. But collecting data does not drive the business forward. You have to do so much more than that. If you are in that camp where you are just collecting data, now is the time to think bigger and start working with other teams. If you are on that customer insights team, start asking questions about what is happening with the data you collected and with the insights you found. What actions are being taken? How will those actions impact your overall organizational success?

Fourth, *remain rooted in reality*. There are many ways to think about your customer experience strategy, but I strongly encourage you to be realistic. For example, do you have the buy-in that you need? Do you have the resources? Do you have the budget?

In my experience, I have not seen any two CX teams that look exactly the same. I have not seen any set of goals that look exactly the same. It will take some work to get to a strategy that makes sense for your organization. But that's why keeping the guidelines highlighted by the four questions above front of mind can be helpful. They can help you make your case in a way that is logical and that ties to the people who really need to buy into the strategy.

Also, as you begin working on your CX success strategy, recognize that there is often no single CX team within an organization. Instead, you may have a voice of customer (VoC) team, an experienced design team, a customer advisory board, or even CX teams within each business unit. Ideally, these various groups will collaborate to create an overarching CX Success Blueprint for the entire organization. Even if you're a team of one, defining CX as a strategy and defining what success looks like will help you prioritize. I urge you—don't skip this step! Don't let your definition of success be a list of tactics that others have assigned to you.

Success Blueprint: Five Steps to Defining Your Strategy

I am now going to introduce you to what I call the CX Success Blueprint. As with the CX Mission Statement, the CX Success Blueprint will capture your strategy in a succinct, specific, and clear way. It will act as a guide for moving forward. This blueprint is the foundation for your success as a customer-focused leader. You can't build your strategy without a solid foundation.

Whereas your CX Mission Statement is an aspirational, emotionally driven statement, your CX Success Blueprint is a business-focused strategic document. It functions much like OKRs or KPIs in organizations that use those to set success parameters. This blueprint is designed to help you prove the return on investment (ROI) that any organization requires.

The CX Mission Statement is about the *why*. The CX Success Blueprint is about the *what* and the *how*.

As with the CX Mission Statement, the CX Success Blueprint is constructed through a series of five steps, with each step culminating in a clear fact that will be inserted into a template. This process is another way to walk through the exercise of thinking strategically about CX and how it fits into your organizational goals.

The five steps are:
- *Identify your top five organizational goals.* Customer experience should serve your organization's larger objectives.
- *Identify the top goal for the key stakeholders in your organization.* Understand not only what's most important for organizational success but also what motivates your organization's leaders to act.
- *Determine your organization's top CX-specific outcomes.* Getting clear about where to focus your CX efforts becomes easier when you see how organizational and individual leadership goals overlap.
- *Choose metrics to measure.* Metrics help measure progress toward your goals. But you have to choose metrics that will give a picture of the transformation you're seeking. (These aren't just feedback metrics either!)
- *Put it all together.* Create a statement that's easy to share and reference.

Let's now review each step in more detail.

Step 1. Identify Your Top Five Organizational Goals
In this first step, you are going to review your overall vision and list the five top goals of your organization. I say five because I don't want you to have twenty. Such a list would

not serve you here. So put on your detective hat and think about what will have the most meaning, what your shareholders care about, what everybody cares about the most. Start there.

For example, one of the top goals of a large enterprise company might be to seek increased market share. A start-up is more likely to be focused on customer acquisition. They need to grow their customer base. On the other hand, a company in a fast-growing stage might be focused on how to increase efficiencies internally and improve customer sentiment and retention.

Top goals depend on the contextual factors of the company. But in all cases, they must be specific. "Increase revenue" is vague as a goal. "Increase revenue by 10 percent" is specific. Since organizational goals are often vague, it is your responsibility to translate the vague goal into specific goals by asking yourself, *What does this really mean, and how can the work that we do impact these goals?*

For example, if you are in an organization with vague goals overall, think about the specific steps you'll need to take to achieve something of impact. Conversion rates are a good place to consider. *Conversion* can mean many things, so get clear on where those conversions need to happen. Improving how often a customer uses your product can lead to "stickier" customers. So if your organization is tracking usage rates and looking for more conversions, think about how CX efforts could drive that. For example, if you believe a better mobile experience would drive more conversions, then consider how your CX efforts could help that initiative. Do you need more customer data to understand if it will have an impact? Would customer journey mapping help your mobile development team see things from the customer's perspective? Get specific. What do you need for that to happen? Maybe you require a budget for an outside consultant or a new tool.

With each organizational goal, ask yourself if CX initiatives could help the overall organization achieve that goal. Then start brainstorming on what it will really require in the context of your CX Success Blueprint.

Step 2. Identify the Top Goal for Key Stakeholders in Your Organization

It's important to consider why we're thinking about stakeholders. Your blueprint needs buy-in, executive sponsorship, and investment. While stakeholders for your entire customer experience program will certainly include frontline employees, customer service agents, and customers, that's not where we are right now. Focus on leaders. This will definitely include the C-suite. It might also include your immediate boss, other team leaders, or key skeptics you want to win over; but your C-suite is a good place to start. What do they care about?

Typically, leaders in the C-suite will have different goals. That's what makes companies run. For example, one can always expect a little bit of friction between sales and marketing. Or on one side you will have the CFO who wants to cut expenses, and on the other the CMO who is requesting more marketing investments.

You want that natural friction in your organization. But when looking at the C-suite leaders as individuals, you want to think about what you could do as a customer experience leader that could serve *all* your leaders—including potential opponents such as your CFO and your CMO. What if, for example, you developed an initiative that cut expenses and improved revenue? Many of your C-suite leaders would be happy.

As you consider your C-suite leaders as individuals, think about what is really motivating them. What are they judged on as leaders? What are their motivations? You have some leaders in the C-suite who are buying into a CX strategy already. They are the ones who give you the nods as you do your executive briefings. They want to earnestly show up for customers. If you have access and a good relationship with these leaders, reach out and ask them about their goals and what is most important to them. Explain that you want to make sure you are focused on the right part of the customer experience so that the outcomes match what they believe is most important. Believe me, they will sit up and take notice of your interest.

I was working with a customer experience leader who realized they hadn't really thought about the goals of individual leaders at all. We sat down and started brainstorming for each leader, just writing out names and titles and thinking about what really motivated them. "Kathy, CMO.

What is most important to her? Stan, CFO. What motivates him?" This is a great exercise because it forces you out of your own role and your own responsibilities to think about how you can relate to these leaders, show them empathy, and actually show up for them in the same way you want to show up for your customers.

This unique exercise will open your eyes a bit to some of the things you perhaps hadn't thought about before. Say Stan, the CFO, wants to cut expenses. How can customer experience actually help cut expenses? If you can answer that question and make a case for it, then other people will appreciate those outcomes even more—which is another benefit of this exercise. In many cases, improving the customer journey proactively creates less need for *reactive* customer service. Fix the problem before it happens. That lowers service costs for the organization.

Once you have results, you can consult your notes and say, "Hey, CMO Kathy, we did increase our word-of-mouth referrals. We initiated a formal referral program, and we were able to increase the number of customers in a year." Once again, this builds the buy-in you need.

The role of a customer experience leader is unique because you have to build relationships with everybody. You have to be everybody's friend and get that buy-in, because CX is a team sport. You cannot deliver results without other people. Understanding those other leaders can be a great help in moving forward. It's a great feeling to discuss your customer experience plans with the C-suite and see the chain reaction of smiles and nods because you are speaking their language! If they can see themselves and their own goals in the blueprint, the chance that it sits on a shelf plummets.

Step 3. Determine Your Organization's Top CX-Specific Goals

Now that you know your organization's goals and your leadership's goals, your next job is to do the work of recognizing and identifying how these two sets of goals correlate. The core questions here are: What is the overlap between our organizational goals and our individual leadership goals, and what specific outcomes support both?

This is the formula you can use: Organizational Goals + Leadership Goals = Specific Outcomes

It looks like simple math, but it's not. CX math is harder! We have to apply the unique vision, goals, and nuances of our organization to determine what should be included in this equation.

There is typically quite a bit of overlap between what you are trying to do for the organization and what your leaders care about the most, which leads to specific outcomes. For example, let's say you have been tasked by a leader with getting more qualitative feedback from your customers. Now you have to think, *What will that actually do for the organization?* Perhaps the qualitative feedback can lead to bigger goals: an increase in referrals, reduction in costs, or more market share.

However, before you can start collecting that qualitative feedback, you need a plan for what will be done with it. In other words, you need to set a feedback *strategy*, and that includes having the right teams available. You need buy-in from the digital team, for example, if you are collecting feedback on the digital experience.

Make sure you have the right resources, the right tools, the right opportunities, the right buy-in, and the right planning in place if you want to successfully achieve what the organization wants and what the leaders want.

Not All Goals Need to Correlate

Not every organizational and leadership goal needs to correlate or have a CX-related outcome. In some cases, they simply won't. For example, maybe the organization has a sustainability goal that 10 percent of all the organization's materials be renewable—a goal shared by several leaders in this organization. Customer experience may not have much to do with such a goal. But challenge yourself. You may be overlooking ways that customer experience does contribute to those goals. I encourage you to dig deep here! The correlations that are hidden at first can end up being the most fruitful.

For example, you might know that sustainability is important to your customers; maybe they've been asking for certain things. Have a cocreation session with customers and your ESG (environment, social, governance) team to discuss what would be the ideal renewable product. The bottom line: Think big while remembering that you may need to take baby steps.

Goals in Action

Let's look at a concrete example. One of your organizational goals is to earn 10 percent more of the market. Your leadership goal comes from the CEO, who constantly says, "Our best customers come from referrals—let's get more!"

Where do these goals correlate, and what CX outcomes can serve them?

To answer these questions, you need to break down the original goals. For example, how do you increase referrals? One way is to increase customer happiness, since customer happiness increases the likelihood of referrals. So how do you know if you are (A) increasing customer happiness and (B) increasing referrals? CX metrics tend to focus on feedback.

You then correlate increasing metrics (such as NPS or customer satisfaction rates) that can have an impact on referral rates. Finally, you track customer churn rate to show that improving customer retention, an outcome of customer happiness, leads to a gain in the market share.

There are many ways to slice and dice metrics and outcomes; what's important is to be clear on what you're tracking and why.

The goal of a CX Success Blueprint is to help you define what success looks like *and* help you measure your progress in getting there. If you track only feedback metrics, it's easy to lose sight of the business results you're *really* aiming for. Happy customers are great, but your organizational bottom line wants happy customers who *stay longer, purchase more,* and *refer friends*. Thinking this way about how traditional CX metrics translate into business outcomes helps you prioritize the right actions and efforts.

Sometimes, CX teams are put in a situation where the organizational goal is the greater use of a CX tool or tactic. For example, the organization might want increased use of its customer relationship management (CRM) capabilities. That in itself is not a CX outcome. The way to approach this type of organizational goal is to think about *why* you have a tool like CRM in the first place and how the organization benefits from it. The answer is that CRM allows your organization to provide more personalized experiences and track your customer's journey so you can deliver more value along the way. You can therefore create goals around CRM use and use those in your CX Success Blueprint.

For example, if you increase adoption of CRM, offer more personalized experiences, and have more customers make it all the way through the customer journey, the organization will gain *more market share*. If you have happier customers, you will incur *lower service costs*. But this won't happen overnight. So connect your baby-step goal with the *why*. Your goal might be to achieve 5 percent more adoption within a year. That goal should connect to the larger goal of serving customers more personalized experiences to increase customer retention rates, leading to more revenue.

If your CX team has established the goal of using a particular tactic more, reverse engineer as I did and think about why you employ that tactic in the first place. Always go back to the big *why*. This is where leaning on your CX Mission Statement can help. Will using the tactic more regularly help you live your mission? It might, if it means showing up more consistently for your customers.

All of this is going to take a decent amount of brainstorming. Start looking at what really matters, what will have the most meaningful outcomes, and how you can make your case. It won't always be easy or happen quickly. I have seen CX teams emerge from this process with so many messy whiteboards, so many messy notebooks, and everything else—but also realistic, meaningful CX outcomes. And the act of thinking through these big questions leads to clear outcomes that can help you prioritize your actions and defend your work!

Step 4. Choose Metrics to Measure
Now comes the time to choose your metrics. Here are some key questions you need to answer during this phase of the strategy development process:

How can we measure this in a meaningful way?
Let's say your organization and its leaders want to increase qualitative feedback from customers. But how can this qualitative feedback be measured to ensure that it is valuable for organizational goals?

Are there challenges, questions, or obstacles to defining the right way to measure?
Measurement—let's take net promoter score (NPS) as an example—can be tricky. A CX leader often does not have influence, authority, or accountability over the actual parts of the customer journey that need to be changed or improved. You need to have a plan for how you will influence (in this example) NPS and why that will drive the business forward.

What are the next steps to define how we measure success?
This is key. You want to find the way to track success around what's most important to achieve your desired specific outcomes. There are different methods and schools of thought for measuring customer experience. Net promoter score was considered the best for quite a while. Today, even Fred Reichheld, who created NPS, says it has been overused, abused, or misused. (Reichheld recently released a book called *Winning on Purpose*, which introduces a 2.0 version of NPS, and there's already debate about this new and improved metric.)[1]

The Right Metric
In contrast, customer satisfaction rate is sometimes the right metric. Customer effort score is another. You also don't want to ignore behavioral data and operational data, which can give you real information about whether the customer experience is working and how to improve it. Usage

CHAPTER 3

rates, contract renewal rates, on-time delivery . . . we need to get to what we really want to know. The bottom line: There is no one blanket, magical metric, so don't look for one!

The best metrics to use will vary depending on your specific goals. Among the metrics that can be valuable, look for indicators of

- Happiness
- Referrals
- Retention
- Sales
- Complaints
- Customer reviews
- Employee referrals
- Fewer service requests
- Repairs needed
- Refunds provided
- Product usage rates
- Loyalty program data

Get creative! Data doesn't just mean feedback metrics. It means operational data and behavioral data. Sometimes a good metric is simply a binary choice. Did we achieve this thing? Yes or no. Some goals might involve deploying new tools or building new data sets. That can take a lot of effort and investment. Start with your why. Then choose the best possible metrics to say whether you were successful. That's the magic metric—the one that can tell you and others about your success.

Too Much Data?

One question you may have is whether there comes a point when you are collecting too much data. My answer is no. I don't put a cap on how many data points to collect because this process is so contingent on various factors. That's why a dashboard approach might be the best feedback strategy. Such a dashboard would include all the right information that will help you move forward—including feedback metrics but also operational metrics, relational metrics, transactional metrics, and more general data points as well.

We are also in the age of artificial intelligence, which can help sift through massive amounts of data to reveal patterns, trends, and early indicators. This is a powerful tool, but the data has to be set up the right way. As of this writing, I see a lot of great ways to use AI, though many organizations simply don't have the data readiness to truly tap into its power. If you have the ability to lean on AI, it can find the needle in the haystack of data. Just make sure you are examining the right haystack and seeking the right needle!

The data you need depends on what you are collecting and where. If you're just looking to measure your performance delivery, you might want to look at customer satisfaction rate—but you want to look at it right in that moment. The quantity of data is not the issue; plus, we have all these amazing tools that can slice and dice data a zillion ways in a heartbeat. There's no reason to restrain that capability. The important parameters are how you look at the data, how you interpret it, and how you act on it. In other words, be thoughtful about why you're collecting the data in the first place.

Step 5. Put It All Together
In this last step, you are finally creating the actual CX Success Blueprint by putting the information you have worked hard to acquire into a single statement as shown in the template below.

> Our organization will be dedicated to achieving these Customer Experience Outcomes: ***[Specific Outcomes]***.
>
> These outcomes serve our broader organization goals, including: ***[Relevant Organizational Goals]***.
>
> They also serve the goals of our leadership, including: ***[Relevant Leadership Goals]***.
>
> We will measure success of these outcomes through these metrics: ***[Metrics]***.
>
> Our outcomes, goals, and metrics are realistic and attainable.

CX Success Blueprint Template

This is very similar to what we did for the CX Mission Statement. Of course, you are going to make this template yours, but this will help you structure what you've collected, discovered, and developed.

Here's an example of a modified CX Success Blueprint for a client that I worked with, with identifying details removed. Note that outcomes, goals, and metrics are indicated in bold. You'll also see the CX Mission Statement is at the top. This is by design. We want to connect the way we define success back to this mission.

CX Mission Statement

Our customers live and work with ease and confidence because we proactively ensure they feel valued along every step of their journey.

CX Success Statement

Our organization will be dedicated to achieving these CX Outcomes:

- Customers trust our bills as a recurring touchpoint

These outcomes serve our broader organization goals, including:

- Easy to do business with
- Serving our community at every level

They also serve the goals of our leadership, including:

- Operational excellence to be an industry leader
- Deliver financial results
- Maximize adoption of assistance programs and self-service channels

We will measure success of these outcomes through these metrics:

- Billing quality, accuracy, and timeliness along with number of complaints
- Enrollment rates of eligible customers into various payment assistance programs

Our outcomes, goals, and metrics are realistic and attainable.

CX Success Blueprint

CHAPTER 3

This organization says it will be dedicated to getting customers to trust their bills as a recurring touchpoint. That outcome might not be one you would expect, but for them, this was a big deal. Their billing was a pain point in their customer journey, something that came up again and again, and they were losing customer trust as a result. So this was a very meaningful outcome for them, something they had to fix. That's why it is a lynchpin of their CX Success Blueprint.

You can also see how this outcome served their broader organizational goals, including being easy to do business with and serving their community at every level. The outcome also served the leadership, who were looking for the operational excellence to be an industry leader, to deliver financial results, and to maximize adoption of the programs they had rolled out already.

You might have been expecting to see typical customer feedback metrics as the main reported metrics, as they often do appear. In other cases, however, the metrics listed in this space will focus on whether the organization achieved its goals. In other words: Did we do it? Do we actually have the tool? Was it rolled out effectively? Do we have the people and the tools we need to take that next step? In this case, billing was a significantly tough part of the customer journey. So billing quality, accuracy, and timeliness are the first metrics on the list of successful outcomes. These metrics tell the organization whether they fixed what was broken.

If the goal were something such as the greater adoption of the CRM, the success metric would not reflect an accomplishment (e.g., billing issues resolved) but rather an activity (i.e., how many more people are now using the CRM).

Customer experience can become overwhelming because there are so many points of input. Many leaders believe everything involves customer experience because everything impacts the customer in some way. The goal of the CX Success Blueprint is to protect you, making sure you are not taking on too much and also that you are actually delivering for your organization.

Moving into Action

Now that you have a strategic plan for your CX Success Blueprint, here are five questions to test whether this plan is ready to do its job.

- Are you able to measure your progress?
- Do your measurements and metrics actually support overall goals?
- Will your leaders support this?
- Do your goals align with your mission?
- If someone outside of your team looked at the CX Success Blueprint, would they know what to measure? Would they know what success looks like?

If you answer any of these questions with a no, then you need to go back to working and reworking your CX Success Blueprint.

CHAPTER 3

Once you have the final draft of an effective CX Success Blueprint, the next step is to move into action—the blueprint doesn't fulfill its purpose of guiding the actions needed to bring your CX Mission Statement to life until you begin to take action.

To gain momentum for action, begin by writing down your action steps in order. What's the very first thing you are going to do? Then what will you do next? Be specific. Simply saying "measure feedback" is not good enough when the first step is actually "determine what to measure." And be equally specific about timing: "This year, we are going to do this."

One final piece of advice: Some leaders will review and update their CX Success Blueprint once a year—a bit like an organizational spring cleaning. How often you update yours should depend on your overall organizational vision and goals. You might have a three-year plan, for example. Your CX Success Blueprint should reflect that same timeline. You can certainly have milestones along the way, but the more closely you can align this with your bigger goals, the better.

Your CX program is working when your CX Mission Statement is infusing every action taken within your organization and every moment that you're serving your customers. The CX Success Blueprint will help you take the right actions—and gather the right metrics to demonstrate that you are living your CX mission.

Ask your team to define *their* goals—at least one of them—around the CX Success Blueprint. At your team meetings and one-on-one meetings, this can become part of your overall evaluation of how things are going. It's truly amazing what happens when you stay focused on what really matters.

So keep it on hand and review it often! Experience works if you work it!

CHAPTER 4

KNOW YOUR CUSTOMER'S TRUE JOURNEY—THE CUSTOMER JOURNEY MAP

Let's say you have a clear idea of your CX mission, and you know you want to focus on CX as a strategy to achieve better business outcomes and establish clear goals. You've defined your mindset and established your strategy.

Now what? Many leaders I've worked with find that it's this moment when they look around at their process maps, org charts, and KPIs only to realize they don't really know where the customer experience is breaking down. How can you prioritize what to fix, improve, and innovate without understanding what's really happening with customers to begin with?

This is where customer journey mapping can be a powerful tool.

I should mention that this is where some teams start. If you aren't quite sure what the journey looks like, or if you don't have strong buy-in for a full customer experience strategy, journey mapping can be a great way to engage others and find some immediate priorities.

In an ideal world, the CX Mission Statement and CX Success Blueprint would guide the mapping by answering questions like "What should we map first?" and "What are our mapping goals?" But in the real world, sometimes you just have to get started!

Wherever you find yourself, remember that it's easy to bounce from one thing to another in customer experience leadership. It's easy to think, *If we just fix this*... or *Maybe let's try this*... and then find yourself playing customer-issue Whac-A-Mole without really knowing where you're going. That's why I personally like to define a true strategy first. But some teams simply aren't ready for that. If that's the case, customer journey mapping is a solid first step with tangible outcomes.

What Do You Mean by *Map*?

Let's start at the beginning: What is a customer journey map? It's typically defined as a visual representation of your customer's journey through all the interactions with your company. And while that's a fine description, I've seen a similar challenge in many organizations. They focus on the map as the goal. But that's not the goal. The map, when done well, is a *tool* to help you achieve other goals.

Focusing too much on making this big, beautiful piece of frame-worthy design doesn't really serve your purposes. The whole point of a customer journey map is to understand the perspective and actual experience of your customers in their interactions with your organization. What are the goals they're trying to achieve? What are they feeling in the moment? What are the obstacles and the points of friction along *their* journey? The process of mapping helps you see things that can be easy to miss from your position inside your organization. Let's face it: We experience the world only from our perspective. In the trenches in your organizations, you're planning new processes and rolling out new products, but you don't have the perspective of the people who you are delivering to. It's virtually impossible to see the customer journey from your customer's perspective. A customer journey map can give you that perspective.

Let's be clear: Your customer's experience starts way before they become a customer and ends well after the sale. But sometimes it's best to refine which part of the journey you're really seeking to understand.

Why Journey Map?

The first reason is to find *points of friction*—those points in the customer journey where you are erecting barriers or complications that prevent customers from achieving what they want to achieve. You can also leverage journey mapping to *uncover duplication of efforts*. I've seen this happen many times. A cross-functional team begins a journey mapping exercise, and soon the member of one team says to members of another team, "Wait, you're doing that? We're doing that too. You're doing this research, but we have a whole team over here doing the same." By looking at the customer journey from the holistic perspective of what is actually happening with the customer, you can uncover the operational inefficiencies and duplication of efforts that happen in organizations all the time.

You can also use journey maps to stress-test new *processes*, *products*, and *services*, thinking about where they actually fit into your customer's journey.

Finally, journey mapping allows you to *envision long-term changes* to improve the experience for all customers. This is where you get into ideal customer journey mapping.

Why Customer Journey Mapping Might Fail

Sometimes customer journey mapping fails.

The first reason, as I mentioned, is that *the journey map is treated like a deliverable*. You think to yourself, *We need a journey map. Okay, we've got a journey map. Check, move on.* The journey map is not the goal. The goal is the wealth of insights that you find from working on understanding your customer's journey.

Another sure explanation for failure is that *you let a technology such as customer relationship management software drive the process.* Instead of reviewing a customer's journey from that customer's perspective, you're trying to fit square pegs into the round holes of your CRM or other software. Your technology and data are definitely part of the journey mapping process, but they shouldn't be the drivers.

Another reason for failure is when *you ignore certain parts of the journey.* When you're looking at the journey, don't forget that people live whole lives. Customers are real people. Don't remove the interaction with your organization from the real world. How are people experiencing the customer journey within the greater journey of their lives? For example, customers don't just "call customer service" as a complete interaction. Think about what that actually requires. They are calling because they need something. They have to find out how to call, potentially interact with an automated system, wait on hold, and so on. Get real about your customers and their real lives. They don't think about your brand nearly as much as you do ... they're just trying to get something done!

Finally, journey mapping can fail when *organizations look at journey maps as things and not as tools to drive change.* The accomplishment is using that journey map to make changes and improvements.

A Visual Representation and a Tool

If you do a quick Google search, you will find a number of different versions of journey maps similar to the one shown on the next page.

It's important to understand that a journey map is a visual representation and a tool. Using the map as a tool to make change is the key to your success as a CX leader.

There are many visual variations of this tool. Some journey maps resemble cartoons and walk through the various

EXPERIENCE IS EVERYTHING

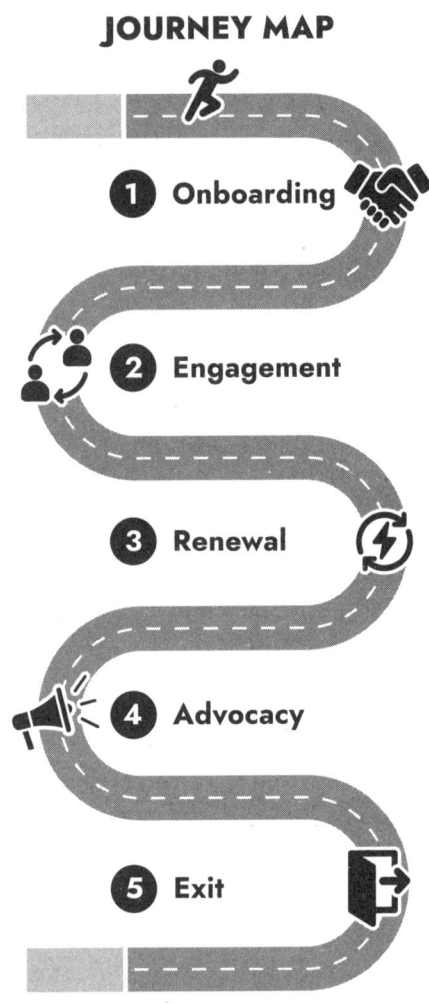

Basic Journey Map

processes in a very animated way. Some of them are more linear, like spreadsheets. The potential manifestations of your customer journey map can reflect the resources at your disposal or the culture of your organization. Think about what works in your organization and what your goal is. If your goal is to present a rational argument for change, something more linear and detailed might fit the bill. If your goal is to socialize what your customers are truly experiencing, you might want something more emotive.

The marketplace, competitive landscape, product updates, and your customer's expectations are never stagnant. A limitation to traditional journey maps is that they tend to reflect a moment in time. The ideal journey map is ongoing and interactive, reflecting the changes in today's world. Luckily, some new, AI-driven technology (like journey orchestration tools and customer management platforms) can help you connect journey mapping with real-time customer feedback data and operational metrics. These can help you identify, with data, where improvements would have the biggest impact. These are powerful tools. Yet many organizations simply aren't capable of that level of journey mapping. Their data lives in silos. They don't collect the right measurements. Or they simply don't have the resources or budget to invest yet. If you have the options, I encourage you to explore what's available in dynamic journey mapping. But if you aren't quite ready for that, the act of journey mapping, even in low-tech ways, can still help you find valuable and important information.

Start Small

Don't be tempted to overcomplicate the journey map. Even the basic journey map on page 102, which is very low tech, can work. Think about what is going to work in the context of your organization. What do you have the resources for? What do you have the time for? What do you have the ambition for? Answering these questions will prevent a customer journey mapping initiative from quickly becoming too unwieldy. In fact, the best approach is to start small.

I've seen many huge, bloated journey maps that don't actually do anything. These maps live in tech platforms that often offer layer upon layer of views. Some are printed on big, laminated boards and cover multiple walls. They are impressive! Yet I've seen many systems and wall boards collect figurative and literal dust as artifacts instead of action drivers.

These comprehensive mapping tools become cumbersome and challenging to use—usually because the journey has changed by the time anyone gets to the insights. We live in a fast-paced world. Before you start, think about which part of a journey you're most curious about. Is there a persona, a specific customer segment that you want to look at carefully? Do you want to understand how customers are interacting with a certain part of the product suite?

Knowing your scope and goal before you start is critical to success. Otherwise, you will become a cartographer of the entire ecosystem at your organization. Start with the end in mind: What do you want to know to drive the right outcomes?

It's vital to find the right scope for your journey map, which begins with thinking carefully about your goal. If you know there's a problem at a certain place in the customer journey and you want to alleviate the problem, then that goal can define your scope. What is the journey like for onboarding? What is it like when customers are trying to renew? You can find parts of your journey that are specific and important to your organization, and doing so will zoom the scope in a little bit. Without a reasonable scope, journey mapping can get overwhelming and will literally lead you nowhere.

What a Journey Map Is Not

In describing what a journey map is not, let's start with the organization's perspective. A journey map is not a description of the customer journey from the organization's perspective. A journey map is always from the customer's perspective.

It is very easy to slip into thinking about what we know from within. Journey mapping might start with the intention of getting into the customer's perspective, but when you describe what your customers are thinking and feeling, you find yourself saying, "Well, I think they are thinking _____." That isn't close enough to the customer. If everything on the journey map is from the customer's perspective, then the *I* will never be you. Translating things to your customer's perspective with *I* statements can be very powerful. So your journey map wouldn't say, "Marketing sends an email." It would say, "I receive an email with an offer."

A journey map is also not a process map. I see this often. The team starts with a customer journey map, but it quickly becomes a process map. It's a map from, once again, *your* perspective within the organization. For example, one of the items on a journey map might be the importance of "inspection criteria." Only the organization needs inspection criteria. Customers don't talk like that. They don't think like that. That's not what they're dealing with. Take a step back and think about what *the customer* is experiencing. What is the pain point that the customer is trying to solve? What emotion are they feeling?

And don't get me started on your corporate lingo and acronyms. They should not be included on a customer journey map. Your customers don't care about your jargon and certainly shouldn't be required to know your acronyms. If you're speaking *your* lingo, you're not on *their* journey.

Another common mistake is to create a journey map according to your organizational chart. I see this most often with how the phases of the journey are defined. If the phases are labeled as "marketing" and "business development," then it's set up according to your org chart and departments, not how the customer is actually moving through their journey. Your customer experiences points in their journey around deciding, thinking, feeling, and experiencing—not marketing and business development. A journey map should flip the script and document everything from that outside-in perspective.

By now you have a CX Mission Statement and a CX Success Blueprint. Use those to guide you. What is most important to your organization? What are your goals in the blueprint? How could journey mapping help you meet those goals? Use your CX Mission Statement to evaluate whether the journey map is working or not. If a customer is waiting a long time for a delivery, for example, is that living up to your mission of always being there when your customer needs you? Think about this customer journey in the greater context of what your customers are doing and what your organizational goals are.

Basic Steps of a Customer Journey

In any customer journey, there are basic steps, as shown below.

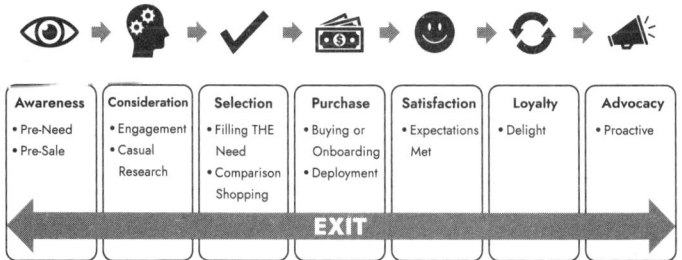

Customer Journey Basics

However, every customer journey map has to be customized to your organization. You might have slightly different steps from those shown on page 107. For example, the software industry might have an onboarding phase, while construction industries and other regulated industries might have a regulation or even a proof-of-concept phase before and during the sales phase. Think carefully about what steps the customer is going through in your industry. More importantly, think about what your customer *expects* as part of their journey.

The basics of a customer journey are awareness, consideration, selection, purchase, satisfaction, loyalty, and advocacy. I call these the basics because they represent the core steps of a customer journey from the customer's point of view. Let's go through each one.

Awareness
A flawed customer journey map may say *marketing* here... but *marketing* is not actually a basic step in the customer journey. The customer isn't thinking, *I'm interested in the marketing phase of this journey.* They are thinking about their needs and how your organization responds to those needs.

From the perspective of the customer, what you might call marketing is, from their point of view, *awareness*—that is, customers becoming aware of your brand... pre-need and pre-sale. One of the things this exercise will do is highlight that you may be taking for granted the many ways customers are referred to you. Maybe you are missing opportunities to increase customer acquisition by simply improving what's already working. In terms of awareness, how does somebody find your organization? Ask that question and then answer as the customer, using *I* statements. *How do I find your organization? Well, I walk by a storefront.* That might be how your organization is building awareness. *I hear about this from my friend.* So, word of mouth. *I ran by a sponsorship banner at a 5K.*

In whatever way your organization is getting out to the market, think about how customers actually experience that awareness from their perspective.

Consideration
We then move into the *consideration* phase. The consideration phase is where the customer might casually research your organization without having a pressing need. A customer might see an Instagram ad for the first time and think, *I've never heard of that brand. It looks interesting.* Tap, tap, scroll, scroll. Over time, the customer becomes more aware of the brand and then starts considering it: *Well, maybe I do have this need.*

Selection
Selection is the step where the customer starts to seriously consider purchasing from you. They might begin to comparison shop. This is where customers start asking themselves, *Will this fill my need? Will this actually help me achieve my goal? Is this the thing that will make me feel the best?* When

customers arrive at selection, you want to think about what will move them to take the next step on the journey: the actual purchase.

Purchase
Once somebody decides to make a *purchase*, they are making a much deeper commitment, a commitment so deep that buyer's remorse can set in very quickly—within forty-eight hours for retail and transactional situations, and within the first ninety days for major business-to-business (B2B) transactions. When you are thinking about how to make the sale better, don't believe that you've won when you get the conversion. Don't have the "we got their money, they got their product, all is good" mindset. Your goal, by focusing on customer experience as a winning strategy, is to look for ways to proactively and intentionally design and deliver great experiences that drive loyalty.

Many customers make a purchase and feel neglected. Once the sale is made, buyer's remorse is about to set in—and it's about this buyer's remorse period that you have to be thinking proactively. For now, your customers need reassurance; they need confirmation they made the right choice. This is a great opportunity to showcase what customer experience can do.

Because reducing the number of cancellations or refunds in the purchase phase of the journey is a win-win for everybody.

CHAPTER 4

Satisfaction

The next phase in the journey is *satisfaction*. If you've met your customer's expectations, they will be *satisfied*. This is one of my least favorite words. Have you ever heard someone in everyday conversation talk about a relationship by saying they were "satisfied" with their significant other? No. It's not a true emotion and nothing to write home about. Satisfaction is the bare minimum. Customers who are satisfied aren't necessarily loyal. They don't really care about your brand. They are not a partner. The transaction with your organization or company was the right thing for them at the time. However, they are waiting to be lured away by competitors. These types of customers go by different names in different industries. I've done some work in the fitness industry, and sometimes we call these "the drifters." They're not quite drifting away yet, but they are ripe to drift soon.

Loyalty

By identifying what's happening in this phase of the journey, you can then create more programs to make them feel more connected and invested in your organization. Discover what you can do to exceed expectations. Because what you want is not just satisfaction but *loyalty*. Loyalty, like each of these phases, is not a stagnant state either. Don't assume that once you've identified ways to get customers to the loyalty phase that they will stay there. You have to keep earning that loyalty.

Advocacy

The ultimate goal is for your customers to reach *advocacy*. You want customers who are sharing their experience with others, who feel like they are almost co-owners of the organization with you. But you can't create customer advocates if you don't deliver on each step of the journey.

> **Making the Map:**
> **Five Guiding Principles**
> **of Customer Journey Mapping**
>
> There are five guiding principles that will help you develop the most effective and valuable map possible. Throughout this process, check in with your CX Mission Statement and your CX Success Blueprint. Will your mapping efforts serve those goals? If the answer is no, it might mean you need to rethink your goal and scope.
>
> **Principle One. Assemble a Cross-Functional Team of Customer Champions**
> You want to involve a diverse team from the start. Ask your champions to help shepherd specific projects to completion and update the map again. Then share what you've learned all over again. This is a wonderful opportunity to build coalitions around customer experience. Journey mapping is an activity that engages other people and

other teams, helping them understand the customer's experience in a different way.

You also want other parts of the organization to understand they're part of the CX effort. Every single employee, whether they're customer-facing or not, influences what happens with customers.

It's true that sometimes you may not be able to pull together a team from different functions. Perhaps you don't have the right resources or the right buy-in. Start where you can—progress over perfection.

Principle Two. Treat *Journey Map* as a Verb, Not a Noun

A journey map is not something that is ever finished, that ever becomes a "thing." Instead, it is a continuous activity, constantly being created and updated and constantly being used. You never say, "Okay, we did marketing once, so we're good for a while." Just like marketing, budgeting, or delivering your products, you need to see mapping as an ongoing part of business.

Principle Three. Map from the Customer's Point of View

One of the biggest misconceptions about customer journey maps is that they're just a series of interconnected process maps. A customer journey map is different in one key way: It's all about the customer's view. In a process map, for instance, you might say, "We send a letter." On a customer journey map, this activity becomes "I receive a letter." You want to shift your perspective so that everything is truly seen from the customer's perspective. You can use data to gain this perspective. Your customers behave in ways that tell you how they feel about their journey. For example, if you are mapping to explore why customers aren't renewing, then understanding and mapping around renewal rates and time frames is important. You can look to earlier phases of the journey and include product usage trends, customer service calls, and more. These data points help illustrate your customer's point of view.

Principle Four. Each Map Should Correspond to a Customer Persona and Objective

A customer journey map designed to serve everybody serves nobody. It becomes overwhelming, and change doesn't happen. Before getting started, have a specific customer persona in mind and know what that customer is trying to achieve along the course of the journey. Based on this knowledge, you can build your first customer journey map—a map that will give you valuable information that you can apply across the organization.

If you need to build up from a single persona, you can always do so. B2B organizations might have different layers to explore or perhaps different customer groups, as they often have buyers who differ from their end customers. It's important to understand both perspectives, so start with one persona. Then you can build on top of it with others. All areas of focus can be explored by building off that first map.

Principle Five. Involve Your Customer
Customer journey mapping is not a guessing game. Mapping the current state of your customer's journey helps identify where changes are needed to get to the ideal state. Use any real customer data you have to better understand what they're truly doing and experiencing at each step. This means going beyond collected data to bring in your customers whenever you can. Create the opportunity to ask them, "Is this actually your experience?" Observation work can be part of this process. How do they actually behave when they're interacting with your products and services? Behavior observation is often overlooked by the customer experience industry, but I believe part of the work we do is anthropology and sociology—understanding how people behave in certain circumstances. Observation in the real world might show you that what your customers tell you, or even what your data might be telling you, does not always convey what is actually happening. Use your voice of customer (VoC) data, operational metrics, and behavioral analytics as ways to include your customer.

Before You Start Mapping the Journey

Before you even start on your journey map, you and your team need to reflect on and accomplish three key steps. First, define your customer journey mapping scope and goals. Second, identify the customers you are talking about and their objectives. Finally, collect and review all available data.

Let's review each of these three key tasks in more detail.

Define Your Customer Mapping Scope and Goals

What should your customer journey map focus on? Here are five steps that will guide you in identifying the scope and goals of your journey map. Even if you already have a problem you're looking to solve or a specific journey identified, these steps will help you align your goals and scope accordingly.

If you are clear on your goals, the scope might become obvious. For example, if your goal is to condense and simplify the onboarding process, then the scope clearly begins before the onboarding process and ends in the phase after onboarding. However, if you are interested in starting a customer journey mapping practice in general and aren't sure where to start, here are some ideas.

Step 1. Ask what your company sells.

Set a timer for three minutes. Ask everyone participating in this exercise to write down the products or services your company sells. This can be a mix of broad and specific products and/or services. You can also include what these products and services do for your customers.

Don't get too overwhelmed. Simplicity is the key. Remember that the goal of a customer journey map is not to build something but to lay out an action plan or strategy. I've seen a customer experience team developing their journey map find an issue that they could fix immediately. If that happens, go ahead and fix it! Don't wait for the journey map to be completed. (Remember: Customer experience is about taking action!)

Step 2. Review your answers to the previous question.
The next step is to review the answers that each participant wrote down. Whenever members of your team hear an answer that they have also written down, ask them to raise their hands. Write down the five most commonly identified items.

Step 3. Discuss which of these journeys is the most straightforward.
Next, referring to the answers from the first question in this exercise, identify as a group which of the items listed are the most straightforward—meaning fewer steps, consistent systems and outcomes, and fewer points of ambiguity. Record the top five answers. This will get you started on your first journey map. You can always add to it later.

Step 4. Choose a common, straightforward scope for your first map.

Review the two lists you have created—the five most cited and the five most straightforward products and services. Are there any answers that appear on both lists? If so, you have found the perfect candidates to serve as the scope of your first customer journey map.

The customer journey map that will emerge from this exercise won't encompass all your products and services. This is intentional. It bears repeating: Simplicity is key. Trying to create a journey map that's too broad can prevent you and your team from taking action and making progress. Consider your first journey map as a template for other future journey maps.

Identify Your Customers and Their Objectives

The next key task before mapping the customer journey is to identify who you are mapping for. Who are your customers, and what are their objectives? The first step is to identify your target persona.

A target persona is a prototype of your customer. Be as real as you can when thinking about who this person is. I suggest removing demographic details (e.g., "Our buyer is typically a sixty-year-old male"). These kinds of data points can limit your thinking and are also outdated. Some organizations won't be ready for this, but if you can remove these types of demographics, your persona might serve you better.

CHAPTER 4

The goal of the persona is not to describe a prototypical customer but to help understand the motivation of that customer—for example, whether this persona is sensitive to shifts in the market or is looking for fresh ideas. Those are the kinds of details that will give you information about what they want in their journey.

Here's an example of a persona we called Penelope for a journey map about hiring speakers for events:

Penelope is an overworked event planner.

Penelope has been in charge of association events for seven years.

Penelope is sensitive to the shifts in the market and looking for fresh ideas.

Penelope knows their budget and values speakers who help promote the event.

Once you've put together a target persona to represent your customers, the next step is to answer these questions: What are customers trying to do? What are their objectives?

When I ask a CX team, "What are your customers trying to do?" I often get an answer such as, "They want to make sure that they have the highest quality whatsit possible." That's not what they want to do. They want the whatsit to *help them do what they want to do.* Customers don't say to themselves, "I want to use that whatsit today." They have a goal in mind, and it's your job to identify, in the context of your whatsit, the customer's goal.

The next question is, "How do they need to do it?"

You can answer this question through what I call micromapping, which means digging down into the details behind the details. For example, you might put as part of the customer journey that "customers call customer service." That's the only thing on the map. But think hard about what that really means. It might mean that the product they bought from you is missing a part, or that they are wondering about the delay in receiving their product, or any number of other negatives . . . because, if they're calling customer service, there's a good chance something hasn't gone right.

"Customers call customer service" also does not explain what happens when the customer calls—a key element in the customer journey. Suppose they call the number on the website, but that number is the sales number. Many companies and organizations are guilty of putting the sales number on the website and hiding the service number. If you're micromapping the customer journey, you would record that your customers call the number available, which is the wrong number, so they get transferred, they get put on hold, they listen to music, they get a recording saying "your call is important to us," they get put on hold again . . .

Think about this as it happens in the real world. Perhaps this is happening on a lunch break, and your customer has to go back to work. Eventually, your customer has to give up, frustrated by the time lost and lack of resolution. All of this is contained in the innocuous phrase, alone on your map, "I [the customer] call customer service." You might have

CHAPTER 4

lost a customer in that action. How do they need to do what they want to do? The answer to that question can be the difference between keeping a customer and increasing that customer's lifetime value or losing a customer and dealing with the subsequent negative word-of-mouth consequences.

This is a good time to discuss the worst phrase in business—especially as you're preparing for customer journey mapping—"It's always been done this way." That is not a legitimate reason for anything. It's a terrible thing to say. If that phrase comes up, you have something to fix.

You may have heard of the Five Whys. This is a common problem-solving technique whereby you get closer to the root cause by asking why five times. I take a similar approach, but I also like to explore alternative situations the customer may face.

The next questions you need to ask in preparation for customer journey mapping all begin with *what if*: What if they need help? What if they can't complete something through that first channel? What if they call us but can't get through? What if the call doesn't solve their problem? You cannot be afraid to keep asking these questions. Customers need reassurance that something works. The last thing you want to do is create anxiety for your customers, and too often I see places in the journey that do just that. No callback creates anxiety. No confirmation creates anxiety. Missing deadlines or delivery dates? That too.

Your goal is the opposite: to reduce anxiety wherever you can. That means reassurance. Throughout your journey map, find opportunities to provide reassurance for customers. If your customers are waiting to hear from you, and there is some kind of delay, at the very least let them know you're working on it. That small step can be quite meaningful in the customer journey. Those are the types of things that will emerge the more you use journey mapping. Because a customer journey mindset will help you realize that there are opportunities to provide little moments of positive, proactive, intentional customer experience.

And finally, in identifying your customers and their objectives, you want to explore *what your customers are thinking and feeling*. There are different ways to do this. Post-its are one very popular way because you can use different colors to signify different things. You can line them up, people can add to them, you can move them around. Another approach is shown on the following page.

This was put together to map the journey of our old friend Penelope. We've identified the situation, the scope, and the goal. Penelope is an event planner and has twelve months to plan a big corporate event.

As you can see, this journey map shows what the Penelope persona is doing, thinking, and feeling. These elements belong on every single journey map.

I often get asked about the difference between thinking and feeling. Thinking is more logical. *I need a speaker.* Feeling is getting into the reality of emotions. *I'm feeling anxious. I'm feeling uncertain. I'm feeling nervous about my job because last time it didn't go well.*

CHAPTER 4

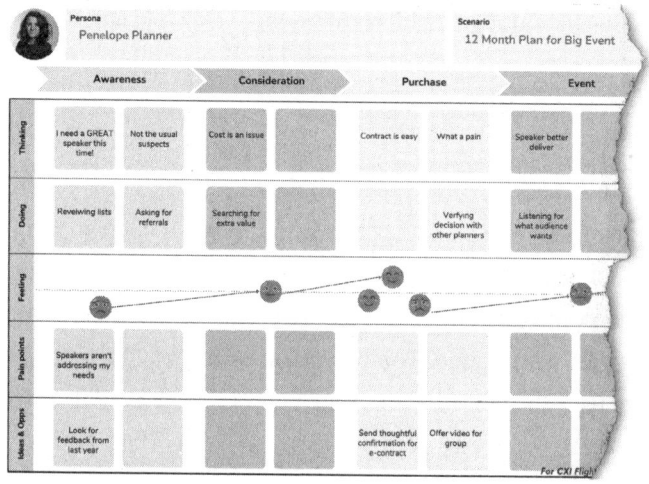

Journey Map

When you walk through what your customers are thinking and feeling, get into the mindset of those *I* statements. They can really help you. Also, beware of words that we use in business that aren't really emotions. Remember, being "satisfied" is not an emotion! Nobody describes their relationship by saying, "Yes, I'm very satisfied."

Find the emotional words that describe their feelings, and then dig into the reasons for those feelings. Are they feeling frustrated? If so, why? Perhaps they're feeling mad because you didn't meet their expectations. Once you've identified the root causes of a negative emotion, you can think about how to respond. If they're feeling frustrated, what can you do to help them feel relieved? If they're feeling anxious, what can you do to help them feel reassured?

There are many different ways to capture the feelings and emotions of your customer, like the emojis we used in the Journey Map on page 123.

Collect and Review Available Data

In the first two steps of preparation for your customer journey mapping, you identified the scope and goals of your journey map and the customer persona for whom your journey map is intended. You're well on your way! The final pre-journey mapping step is to collect and review available data.

When building your journey map, any data you have about your customer or journey is extremely valuable. Data may include voice of customer (VoC) metrics, such as Net Promoter Score (NPS), Customer Satisfaction Score (CSAT), or Customer Effort Score (CES). You can acquire data from qualitative customer feedback from surveys and feedback forms. Existing known systems, procedures, and touchpoints that may be relevant to the particular journey will provide more sources of data.

One of the questions I get asked sometimes is, "What if we don't have any data available?" Well, data is everywhere. Some of it can be formal, like the scores mentioned, but some of it is informal. What do you know customers say about your product? That's data. What about usage rates or buying patterns? That's data too.

Everybody has data. For example, think about your social media and other online channels. Are customers talking about your brand or products online? Try searching

CHAPTER 4

your email archives for product or service names and emotional words. Review contact center recordings or talk to service agents for insights.

Finally, check your existing systems. Even systems that aren't specifically customer focused, such as internally focused process maps, may shed light on how customers move through their journey, where their points of strength and weakness are, and more.

Invite Your Customers—and AI (Within Reason)

Customer journey mapping tools have advanced just like everything else. Artificial intelligence can help with mapping, but be sure you are validating what's happening based on real customers and their stories. AI can certainly speed up mapping efforts and help visualize information. But one of the rewards of journey mapping is staying ahead of customer expectations, which are always changing. AI relies on inputs of data. This can be very helpful if that includes your specific customer feedback, operational data, and so on. But customers, with their humanity and emotions, will always give you a richer, more human perspective of their journey.

To be clear, including customers doesn't necessarily mean including them in journey mapping activities from the beginning. Include customers by including their data, observing them in their real-world journey, and leveraging artifacts such as contact center call recordings, customer videos, product reviews, and social media mentions.

Remember that humans are tricky—it's easy to "lead the witness" if you're not thoughtful about how to include them. It's a great exercise to interview customers about their actual experiences, run through a journey mapping exercise, or validate the journey you create with them.

Some purists will say you can't conduct journey mapping without customers in the room. I humbly disagree. We need to start where we can, with what we have. I believe we can "include" customers by including their requests, their complaints, and their ideas. Once you create a new journey or fix a specific challenge, it's time to check in again. This is where a pilot program or A/B testing can be enlightening.

AI also stirs up controversy with CX leaders. But AI is here, and it's a powerful tool. It can help us aggregate data quickly and help us make predictions based on how customers have already behaved. It can lead us to consider breaking out the phases of the journey differently and can inspire new ways to visualize the journey.

Some tools are now introducing "synthetic data," which essentially allows you to ask questions of "fake" customer groups that AI has created based on your actual customers. This can be a good jumping-off point, but I personally recommend caution in relying on this type of information. We live in a world of nuance, and we, as leaders, need to leverage the tools available to us while still respecting the unique traits of humanity. If something seems too perfect or too crazy, it probably is!

CHAPTER 4

A Few More Pitfalls to Avoid

There are a lot of easy mistakes to make when you don't plant yourself firmly enough in the mind of the customer. Here are a few words of warning.

First, we have described the customer journey as a linear process. But don't believe that people are going to march through this journey as dutiful soldiers, because that's not how customers operate. Your mindset should always be that the customer is in charge; they can exit at any point throughout this process. Therefore, you need to keep them firmly in mind and reflect carefully on what they are trying to do during the journey and what would cause them to drop out. Understand, for each phase of the journey, what is actually going on with the customer. For example, in the selection phase, if they don't get a call back from you but get a call back from a competitor, that might be enough. Always be on the lookout for pain points and opportunities.

Second, don't jump ahead. For example, don't just say, "The customer can order groceries on the app." That's too succinct. How do they find the app? Do they have to download it? Is it something that they have to sign up for? Do they need an account? What if they don't have an account? What if they go through the whole process and they can't get their payment to work? Who do they call? What happens? That's the level of understanding you need to draw out when describing the customer journey. For in such detail, you will find the insights.

Another potential mistake is to fool yourself into thinking about your best customer on their best day. If you take that approach, it's easy to declare, "Our customers love us so much!" We love to think about those customers. Don't. For journey mapping, one of the strongest things you can do is think about your worst customer on their worst day. Who is this person? What are they complaining about?

Your worst customer on their worst day will be giving you information. With this mindset, you might start thinking, *Okay, if our worst customer couldn't find the right mobile app, how would that make them feel? Well, they would be frustrated, they might be angry, they might be disappointed, or they might just say, "I'm moving on to the competitor. I am going to search for a different app."*

It comes back to uncovering the pain points, the exit points—the most valuable data to be derived from customer journey mapping. And the bonus is that by improving the experience for your worst customer on their worst day, you are improving the experience for all your customers!

Finally, it's important to realize which data you might be missing. For example, a company may want to improve its number of transactions. In the observation work they perform as part of their customer journey mapping, they notice that their lines are too long and people are leaving before completing their transactions. The number of people lost to long lines would be an important piece of data for this company.

Making assumptions is an unavoidable part of business—but whenever possible, try to uncover the data that will answer your questions better than any assumptions. One place to start is by asking, "What do customers never tell us?" Most customers are not in the habit of explicitly communicating with the organizations they interact with, especially if they are not contacted by those organizations. Sometimes this lack of communication is unintentional—customers may not necessarily be aware of their behavior or decisions. Many of our actions as human beings are automatic, done without thinking consciously of our motivations or intentions.

Think carefully about how to uncover the data that will help you answer the questions you need to answer with your customer journey map. Thinking about the bigger journey might add to your insights, so collect data about customer behavior *before* they become a customer and *after* the sale has been completed.

The Seven Steps of Journey Mapping

Once you have defined your customer journey mapping scope and goals, identified the customers and their objectives that you want to focus on, and collected and reviewed all the available data, you are ready to move forward and develop your customer journey map. In this section, we'll walk through the seven steps of journey mapping that build on all the work that came before. These seven steps are shown on the following page.

EXPERIENCE IS EVERYTHING

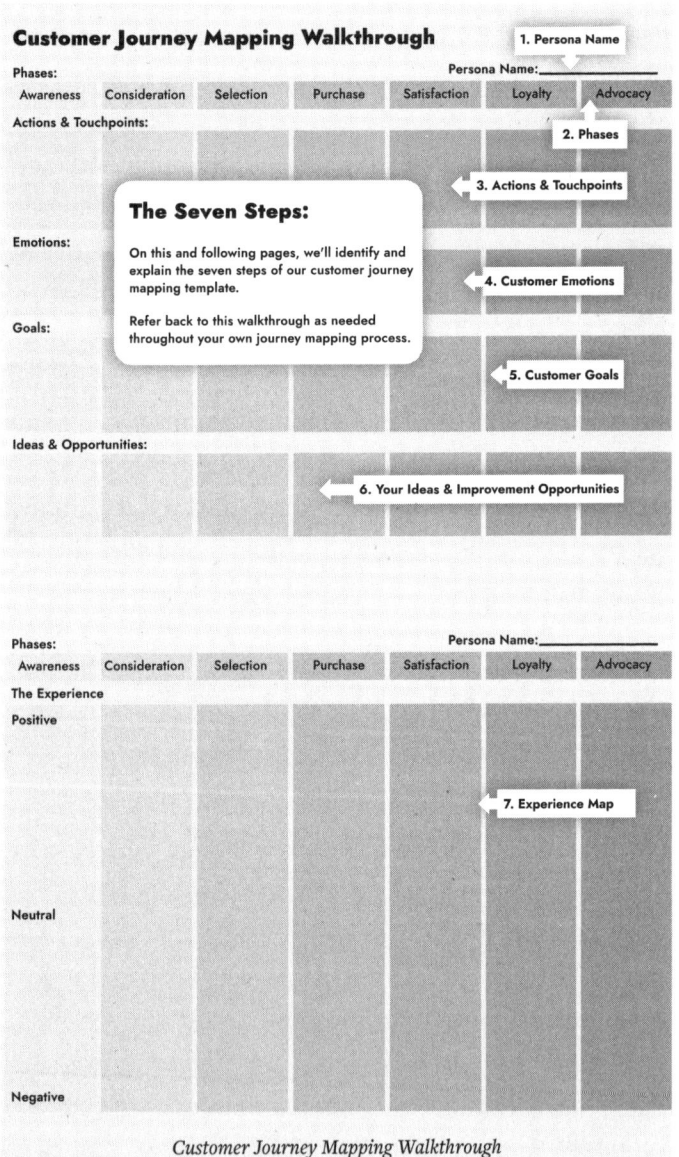

Customer Journey Mapping Walkthrough

Let's quickly review each of these seven steps.

1. Record the name of the specific customer persona you've chosen to build a journey map for.

Make sure everyone involved in the process understands who your persona represents. A note about personas: In today's world, I like to "neutralize" the persona when possible. Indicating gender, age, or even geography can sometimes skew our thinking about who *could* be our customer in the future. The customer of the past is not necessarily the customer of the future, and your goal is to understand their emotions and needs, not their demographics.

2. Develop the phases of the journey your customers undertake.

In the templates on page 130, these phases—awareness, consideration, selection, purchase, satisfaction, loyalty, and advocacy—have been re-filled for you based on the seven basic steps of the customer journey we described earlier. Of course, experienced journey mappers may want to edit the names of those phases to fit the specific needs and contexts of their organization. This is where having a clearly identified goal is so important. Don't get carried away on phases; just zero in on what you want to learn and the phases included there.

3. For each phase, identify the key touchpoints and actions in your customer's journey.

These are often the largest, most significant moments in the journey. However, you could also collect micro-moments. These little moments in the customer journey can have a large impact. The touchpoints you choose to include should be guided by the scope and goals your team established earlier.

4. Explore your customer's emotions during the journey.

What is your customer feeling in each phase? You can use adjectives, emojis, hand-drawn faces, or any other of a multitude of ways to represent these emotions. Just make sure they're unambiguous and meaningful.

5. Identify what the customer is trying to accomplish in each particular step.

What is the best possible outcome of each touchpoint/interaction for the customer? Remember to *keep things focused on the customer*. Your internal goals may not necessarily align with your customer's goals at certain points. That's okay, but for this exercise record the customer's goal.

6. Develop ideas and identify opportunities to improve touchpoints.

Reviewing the sections you've already completed will help generate ideas. Some potential questions that uncover ideas and opportunities include: Where can you make things easier for the customer? When can you acknowledge difficult moments in the journey or make them easier? How can you increase the likelihood that customers reach their goals?

7. Visually plot what customers are feeling throughout each phase of their journey.

It's a chance to record the previously identified customer emotions and display them in a way that's quantifiable and easy to interpret at a glance. You always want to have some sort of emotional map. The Experience Map (page 130) highlights what's positive, what's negative, and what's neutral in the customer journey—revealing where you might want to prioritize your focus.

Remember, you don't have to wait for a big event to do a journey map. Yes, there are robust, beautiful journey maps with all the data; these will take a long time to put together but, in the end, can give you a massive amount of information.

But if you don't have that kind of time and those kinds of resources, take any opportunity you can to develop a simpler, quicker customer journey. As long as you keep focused on the scope and goals that will give you the answers you need, even a relatively quickly prepared

> customer journey map will offer insights that will at least spur on your progress toward better customer experience.

Post-Mapping Actions

Once you have a map, what do you do? I've often encountered CX teams who find themselves at a stopping point once the map is done. They worked very hard on their map. They get compliments on the map from their colleagues and coworkers. But in the end, they are not quite sure that the map is making a difference.

In this section, I describe the specific actions you need to take to ensure that, indeed, the customer journey map in which you and your team invested so much time does make a significant difference for you and your organization. This is the most vital phase of the entire exercise. It bears repeating: *Your goal is not to create a map—your goal is to create a tool that you then use to take action.*

Here are the three actions to take with your customer journey map in hand:
- Identify Moments of Truth and Potential Actions
- Prioritize Actions
- Summarize and Share

Identify Moments of Truth and Potential Actions

The first step is to identify moments of truth—those key moments when your customer is interacting with your company or organization, and it is either going well or not so well

CHAPTER 4

for that customer. These are the moments when the journey is either *made* or *broken* for your customer, depending on whether the moments are positive, negative, or neutral.

For example, let's take your sales process. When they are trying to acquire customers, your salesforce pays special attention to their prospects. When those prospects become customers, however, they suddenly stop receiving the same attention, and they start to feel disappointed with your company. This is a moment of truth, when customers are beginning to feel disappointed; this moment of truth occurs in the handoff between sales and post-sales.

Uncovering moments of truth is both an art and a science. Sometimes, data will provide the answers—or at least clues to the answers. For example, data can show where customers are dropping out of the customer journey or where there are moments of high complaint volume.

Sometimes, however, you have to use some intuition. You might notice a moment of truth where it seems many prospects are deciding not to move forward and buy your product or service. You might conduct some kind of pilot test to determine whether, indeed, this is a crucible moment where you are losing customers.

To work with the moments of truth, you have to begin by first identifying them and recording them, grouping them by positive, negative, or neutral.

Start with the positive ones. You can use the emotions and experience map sections of your journey map as starting points. Look for moments when the experience you deliver exceeds the promise you've made to your customers and for moments when you've anticipated potential customer problems or anxiety and presented solutions proactively.

Then, for each moment that you've identified, try to mark down what made that moment particularly great for the customer. Come up with as many reasons or explanations as you can!

Next, record the key negative moments in your customer's journey as you identify them. Once again, start with the emotions and experience map sections of your journey map. Look for moments where the experience you deliver doesn't live up to the promises you've made to your customers, and for moments when customers often get stuck, frustrated, or anxious. For each of those moments, ask yourself what makes that moment particularly difficult for the customer. Be specific and comprehensive.

Once you have this list of negative moments completed, ask, "Can we do anything about these moments? And will our actions have an impact?" With your journey map completed and your moments of truth clearly identified, it's time to take action. But first you need a plan, and that plan will be based on the list of potential action items that you are now going to generate.

Start with your list of moments of truth and look for:
- positive moments that can be systemized, taught to others, and/or applied to other touchpoints
- negative moments that can be efficiently resolved

CHAPTER 4

When looking to improve the customer journey, CX teams often concentrate on the negative moments of truth. That's understandable. It would seem that addressing those negative moments of truth is the most urgent task at hand. However, it's equally important to look closely at the positive moments of truth as well. Because if something is going really well, you want to ask why. It might be something you can replicate, a best practice you can apply to different parts of the journey. In other words, looking at your positive moments of truth has yielded solutions for the negative ones.

You might ask everyone on your team to record their own answers and then review and discuss together, or you might brainstorm together from the outset. Whatever the approach you take, don't worry about the feasibility of the action items you and your team are generating—because you will review and prioritize those items next.

Prioritize Actions

You now (hopefully!) have a long list of potential actions to explore. But which ones should you prioritize? Start by reviewing your list of potential actions, asking for each:

- What impact will this action have on our business outcomes? Is it worth the investment to fix it?
- How feasible is this? Is it something we could fix quickly, or would it be a long-term diversion?
- What is our CX mission? Does this action get us close to delivering the experience we've promised our customers?

Based on the answers to these questions, record your potential actions on the Journey Map Priority Matrix (see below). The matrix is a great tool to help you isolate the action steps that will have the highest impact and are also the most feasible. Those are the items—the five or six things that you can put in the upper right, high impact / high feasibility quadrant—that you want to start with. You might consider those items your marching orders once you've completed your customer journey map, because they will allow you to make a significant, positive difference.

Next, you should proceed to the upper left, high impact / low feasibility quadrant. You know that these are high-impact items, so you and your team must concentrate on

Prioritize Actions

Journey Map Priority Matrix

High Impact / Low Feasibility	High Impact / High Feasibility
Low Impact / Low Feasibility	Low Impact / High Feasibility

Prioritize Actions

how to overcome the feasibility barrier. First, identify what makes them low feasibility. Perhaps the issue is that you will need to overhaul your technology to implement them. Or perhaps you will have to bring in a new set of employees and managers. Once you've identified the barrier to implementation, you can start to think about overcoming these barriers. Perhaps there are workarounds you can put in place. Perhaps you can make a case for going after short-term objectives first, then considering the longer-term objectives that might require more resources.

As for the low impact / low feasibility group, these are the action items that may not be worth pursuing.

Summarize and Share

You have now built a customer journey map for a specific customer persona and journey. You've identified the high and low points in your customer's journey. You know what you want to replicate and what you want to fix. Finally, you've created a prioritized list of potential action items that can have a meaningful impact. You should be proud of your accomplishment. But there is one more critical step: sharing all your hard work with those who matter.

Remember that your goal is not just to learn about and describe the customer's experience. The goal is to improve it. And you can't do that alone. You will need cross-functional staff support and top leadership buy-in to leverage the knowledge and insight and implement the action plan that has emerged from the efforts of you and your CX team.

The beauty of a journey map is that it is something you can socialize and share. It's packed with information and data, but it is also presented visually—perfect for getting your leadership's attention and generating enthusiasm from other parts of the organization.

There are two categories of audience members you want to attract. The first category: *those who would be interested in the information.* Perhaps your findings or potential actions might affect a particular individual or department. Or perhaps you have identified a high or low point in the customer's journey that stems from the way another department handles things. Maybe your recommendations solve someone's problem. In either of these cases, make sure the interested parties know!

Let's say, for example, that you have identified an issue related to your retail locations. You will probably want to share that with your head of retail, with your facilities team, and with anyone else who could have an impact on what's happening in the retail stores. If, on the other hand, you find problems related to technology that are causing problems for customers, you want to bring in your organization's technology team.

The second category to target: *those with the authority to take action.* These are the people who could make a significant impact in helping you implement your action steps. Who are the leaders you need to champion your ideas and recommended actions? These are your executive sponsors. Getting the required buy-in from decision-makers will be key to getting better results for your organization and your customers.

For example, it's possible the C-suite leader ultimately responsible for the retail function has never heard of the retail store issue you identified. In this case, you want to work with an executive sponsor to get in front of the C-suite and say, "This is what we've learned, and this is what we want to do about it."

This retail example shows how journey mapping can lead to a faster conversation and faster action. And it's more meaningful than just showing a spreadsheet; a customer journey map helps people understand the issues and the stakes.

Many people will be surprised by the insights uncovered; they'll say something like, "This is not the process I thought we had" or "I thought our process was really working." These responses are not surprising given that many of your colleagues are probably viewing everything from the perspective of the organization and NOT the customer. From inside the organization, a faulty process can feel like it's working. But when you show exactly what's happening to the customer and what customers are thinking and feeling and dealing with, their perspectives can be transformed.

Once you've identified whom to share with, you must summarize the work you did, the key findings you discovered from this work, and the recommended actions that emerged from your key findings. Don't just share the final journey map. Instead, summarize how you identified and acquired the information needed to create the journey map, how you used that information to create the final journal that they have before them, and how you used the journey map to arrive at your final recommendations and action steps. This can lead to better understanding and buy-in.

And don't forget—relate this back to your CX Mission Statement and your CX Success Blueprint. Be prepared to answer how this journey and your recommendations are related to the mission and how these efforts will help you deliver on your strategy.

Trying to summarize all the work you've done since you first started the customer journey mapping process may seem daunting. To help with the summarization task, here's a list, in order, of the items that should be included in your summary:

- the scope and goals of the journey map
- a description of your customer persona, including what they are trying to achieve in their customer journey, their emotions and motivations, and some general demographic information
- the sources of the data you used
- highlights of the steps you took to adapt the information into a customer journey map
- some of the best customer moments and worst customer moments as revealed in the customer journey map, as well as potential actions suggested by both the positive and negative moments

CHAPTER 4

- the priority action steps that you and your team are recommending to the organization
- the individuals and the departments with whom you are sharing the customer journey map and its recommendations

The template on the following page shows a suggested form that can gather all this information clearly and succinctly.

In this chapter, you learned how to create a customer journey map. You also learned how to turn that tool into action by identifying the moments of truth, developing potential actions to deal with negative moments of truth, prioritizing the actions you've developed, and summarizing and sharing the customer journey map. The goal is to instill the CX mindset throughout your organization. This is just one tool in your tool kit, but it's a powerful, important one.

The next chapter will describe how to create the culture-first culture in your organization that is vital to reaching your customer experience goals.

Summarize & Share

Our Customer Journey Mapping Process, Results, & Recommended Actions...

Our Scope (Exercise 1)
As a first step, we set out to map a customer journey that was both common and straightforward. The journey scope we chose is _____
_____

Our Customer Persona (Exercise 2)
Next, we selected a single customer persona to focus on.
The customer persona we chose for this customer journey map is: ____
_____

Their main objective within this journey is: _____
_____

Their emotions and motivation are: _____
_____

Their general demographics are: _____
_____

Our Data (Exercise 3)
We used data from the following sources: _____
_____
_____

Template for Summarization Form (Exercises 1-3)

CHAPTER 5

Summarize & Share

Our Customer Journey Mapping Process, Results, & Recommended Actions...

The Journey Map
We build out the journey map by looking at several phases in the customer lifecycle, including pre-sale, sale, and customer phases. For each phase, we identified key touchpoints and customer actions, emotions customers typically experienced, specific customer goals, and opportunities we identified to improve the steps along the way. We also mapped out moments on a spectrum of positive experiences all the way to negative ones.

Moments of Truth & Potential Actions (Exercise 4)
Using our journey map, we recorded the best and worst moments in the customer journey.
Key positive moments include:
  1. _____ because _____ .
  2. _____ because _____ .
  3. _____ because _____ .
Key positive moments include:
  1. _____ because _____ .
  2. _____ because _____ .
  3. _____ because _____ .

Template for Summarization Form (Exercise 4)

Summarize & Share

Our Customer Journey Mapping Process, Results, & Recommended Actions...

Prioritized Potential Actions (Exercise 5)

Using everything we'd learned, we narrowed down a prioritized list of potential actions.

These actions include:

1. _____ .
2. _____ .
3. _____ .
4. _____ .
5. _____ .

Sharing (Exercise 6)

Finally, in order to get broad buy-in, support, and invite collaboration, we're sharing this information with the following individuals and departments: _____

_____
_____
_____
_____
_____
_____

Template for Summarization Form (Exercises 5-6)

CHAPTER 5

A CX CULTURE

Your company's culture can greatly influence your success as a customer experience leader. Sometimes, the concept of culture can feel vague and foggy. However, even if you take tools such as journey mapping or voice of customer, collect all the feedback, and investigate and find the data, the only way you can really take action is if there is cultural commitment in your organization.

Your culture is key to aligning everyone in the right mindset. You need everyone involved to understand the strategy, but none of this matters without the discipline to connect each person's work with successful outcomes. Culture impacts customer experience in ways too numerous to count.

What Is Culture, Anyway?

You and your organization may have decided to adopt a customer-centric culture. That's great! However, creating such a culture requires more work than simply announcing that it's time to think more about customers.

First, you have to determine what makes up a culture in the first place. Culture is a system or collection of beliefs, values, and assumptions. In other words, what do you as an organization collectively believe? Where are you collectively aligned? What are the processes and commitments and truths you agree to abide by for one another?

For instance, one organization might have a culture of speed. They have to be fast; that's what they're all about. Rapid, rapid, rapid. That type of culture might be important for certain industries. Another organization might have a culture of nurturing. Or an organization might have a culture that is focused on results and nothing more. All they care about, all they measure, are results.

Culture creates the environment and vibe of the organization. It is usually defined and communicated by founders and leaders but is also shaped and changed by employees. Whatever its origin, organizational culture can have a significant impact on the success or failure of an organization.

The best cultures respect people as individuals. You see one another. You respect each person's role. Everyone is held accountable. This indicates a good culture, because without universal respect and commitment, levels of success will vary from person to person—and that often leads to resentment and other negative emotions and dynamics. You need empathy and compassion, and you need to recognize one another as individuals to allow people to bring

CHAPTER 5

their whole selves to the organization. With respect and accountability, your organization will get the results it seeks, and people will not only feel successful—they will feel as if they're contributing to the success of the organization.

What Is a Customer-First Culture?

It's nearly impossible to deliver a great customer experience without creating a customer-first culture. The best brands in the world boast cultures that empower employees to deliver for customers. Yet many organizations have cultural legacies focused on short-term goals such as quarterly results. Some product-focused cultures all but ignore the customer experience.

Note that *customer-first* is a term that is often used interchangeably with *customer-centric* or *customer experience–focused*. As you are introducing these ideas throughout your organization, use the language and the nuance that applies to your organization, your industry, and your leaders.

So, what is a customer-first culture? In a customer-first culture, people show up and understand that they have a role to play in delivering the customer experience even if they are not customer-facing. They also understand that creating a customer-first culture requires a cycle of investigation—understanding your customers through observing, collecting feedback, reviewing analytics, gathering the right insights, applying those insights to the priorities of the organization, and taking action. This is a cycle you repeat again and again.

Too often organizations and leaders treat customer culture as if it's fairy dust. (There's that magical thinking again!) Just talking about being customer-centric doesn't make you customer-centric. Your talk needs to be turned into real activities and efforts. You have to have a bias toward action, because that's how you get the outcomes you want. That's how you get results.

Great customer experience is good for the customer, but it also means better business results. And if you want the organization to invest in something like cultural commitment, you need to make a business case for it. You will get the critical leadership buy-in you need only if you are sharing results that matter to your leaders. "Having a great culture is really important to customer experience" sounds fluffy. But if you say you want to invest in the following ways because you know if you deliver better customer experiences, your customers are going to spend more, they're going to refer more, your service costs will go down, and so forth—now you are getting into concrete business outcomes.

So think about what your organizational leaders care about. Think about what is important to your organizational outcomes and build your business case from there. For example, you might say, "A new research report found that customer-centric companies were 60 percent more profitable." As a business owner, I know "60 percent more profitable" would get my attention. Your leaders will want to understand the return on this investment, and the generalized data out there can help them do just that. Something like, "Recent data found that 64 percent of companies with a customer-focused CEO are more profitable" is a real business result linked to a customer-first culture that your leaders will pay attention to.

A customer-first culture is good for customers and means better business results. Customers will spend more, stay longer, and tell their friends about the brand. If metrics like retention rate, lifetime customer value, and new leads from referrals are important to your company, then great customer experience is too.

And let's not forget that happy employees are critical for customer experience success. In today's competitive market, happy customers also mean better employee retention rates, lower hiring costs, and a better employer brand reputation.

How Can You Create a Customer-First Culture?

Because culture is often discussed in obtuse, abstract ways, employees can be cynical about the word. Leaders can sometimes assume their culture is good for everyone when it isn't. And customers can lose trust in organizations that don't have cultures aligned with their values.

You can create a customer-first culture by creating a culture with an engaged, empowered workforce and an authentic, open environment. That's very important. You want a culture that encourages employees to do their best work. You want to create an innovative, future-focused, and adaptable work community intent on solving customer challenges. In an ideal world, the customer experience mission you've carved out will say, "This is who we are." This is who you are in the culture. This is who you are in the employee experience. That is who you are in the vendor experience.

There has to be an alignment between what you're doing for the customer—the promises you've made—and what is happening inside your culture. If you tell customers you want to be transparent and authentic, but you know that's not really happening inside your culture, employees will feel the dissonance! This disconnect will make it much harder for them to deliver on the experience vision you have for your customers.

It all comes back to our three pillars: mindset, strategy, discipline. Everything starts with a mindset, which is then converted into strategy—making a plan for your success—and then having the daily discipline to get the work done, to deliver the strategy through everyday efforts. You can do that only through an aligned, universal vision of what you want for the customer experience. That's why you start with those foundational tools: the CX Mission Statement and the CX Success Blueprint. They help guide the daily discipline of these efforts.

The Four C's of Customer Experience Culture

How can you be sure the culture you want is the culture you have? How can you lead an organization through a cultural transformation? While I can't give you a recipe, I can offer some guidelines based on what I call the Four

CHAPTER 5

C's of a Customer Experience Culture: *Conscience* (which sounds heavy but is really straightforward), *Communication*, *Consistency*, and *Credibility*. A CX culture needs all four to be successful.

Let's look at each of the four C's in more detail. Note that culture is not linear. The tools useful for one of the C's can often be applied to others. Like most things in customer experience (and leadership in general), there is rarely a straight line. It's important to lean into what works at your organization.

Conscience

The first C is *conscience*. Your conscience is what guides your decision-making. It's what guides the actions you take. For example, your conscience tells you not to steal. (Or at least I hope it does!) You will make the decision not to steal, even if the opportunity is there. That's conscience on an individual level.

In culture, we are talking about conscience at the *collective* level—everyone having the same conscience leading to the same decision-making.

If culture is described as "how and why we do things around here," it's the collective conscience of the organization that drives those decisions. Again, this collective conscience is often treated like fairy dust. "Oh, everyone here understands what a great customer experience is!" It's not that easy. Because our individual consciences will vary based on our individual experiences.

To create a collective conscience, everyone in your organization has to speak the same organizational language; everyone has to understand the customer experience that you want to deliver.

The challenge in many organizations is a lack of collective conscience. Employees must make judgment calls on their own or follow policies that are outdated, unfair, or misaligned with the true vision, mission, and values of the organization. Inevitably, the customer experience suffers, and customers lose faith that your organization will deliver what it says it will deliver.

Specific tools will help you with developing a collective conscience. One is your CX Mission Statement. In the CX Mission Statement, you define how you want people to feel when they interact with your brand. You define what you are doing for customers beyond the products and services that you sell. You define how they feel even *after* they have interacted with your brand.

Next, look at the ideal customer journey. If you have the ideal customer journey mapped out, you will be able to see the gaps in your customer's journey in a different way. You can then prioritize bridging those gaps faster and more efficiently.

Finally, you want to truly know your customer, collectively. If you start talking to people and they define the customer differently, that's a red flag in your culture. You have to understand who you are delivering to and what's important to them.

CHAPTER 5

So how do you establish a collective conscience? There are a number of ways.

Socialize the Customer Experience Mission

The first step in establishing a collective conscience is to socialize the customer experience mission. Make sure that you think about how to get your customer experience information out into the greater population. How can you include different teams? How can you make this effort as cross-functional as possible? It's your CX Mission Statement that guides your intentions, actions, and behaviors, and it's important to your culture to communicate about this mission in an ongoing way.

In addition to conscience, socializing the customer experience mission also involves *communication*, *consistency*, and *credibility*.

View Customer Experience as a Team Sport

No one leader can be responsible for an entire culture. A culture evolves and grows based on the actions and ideas of employees—which means that if a customer-centric culture is the goal, each employee must be involved and held accountable for creating and delivering on that customer-centric culture. Leaders must also be involved—for example, through participation in events, communications, or frontline days.

In addition to *conscience*, viewing customer experience as a team sport also involves *communication*, *consistency*, and *credibility*.

Create a Customer-Centric Employee Experience
The brands with the most effective brand cultures are also the ones that use their customer focus as a factor in their decisions. And being customer-centric isn't reserved just for the customer-support or customer-success teams; it is a guiding factor in how to hire, evaluate, and encourage all employees.

Creating a culture focused on customers has to start and end there—with focusing on employees. A culture that aspires to be authentic for customers must live up to that in the employee experience too. People want to live their values, and that includes at work.

Employee journey mapping and other techniques can be used to understand where, how, and when to reinforce the mission. Team members want to deliver their best, and it's critical that the definition of what is best is well articulated and communicated throughout their experience.

This also translates into employee compensation and rewards. Not all organizations are designed to do this right away, so it's important to ensure the right mechanisms are in place. In other words, don't jump into tying compensation to customer-centric measurements until there's confidence in how these are tied together.

Employee journey mapping, employee listening sessions, and 360-degree surveys are techniques that can help, but the first step is to define the experience for employees. What expectations do they have, and what expectations does the overall culture have for them?

In sum, look carefully at the employee experience. Make sure you're including the employees in developing this collective conscience around a customer-centric culture.

In addition to *conscience*, creating a customer-centric employee experience also involves *consistency* and *credibility*.

Communication

If there's one gap in almost every organization, it is usually around the second C: *communication*.

Consider how your internal communications reflect the customer-first culture in your organization. Do these communications mention customers, the customer experience mission, customer feedback, and goals around customer experience?

While leaders must communicate around the mission, it's just as important that employees feel empowered to communicate to leaders about what they see, what's working, and what's not. You want a system in place through which they can share that type of feedback. Organizations have to be very careful that their responses to employee communication are not punitive. Honest communication on behalf of customers should not lead to punishment or retribution.

One of my clients had an annual employee survey (as many of you probably do). If a manager did not score high enough on this survey, they were forced to have a meeting as a team. In this meeting, the team was asked to communicate to the manager what, basically, they didn't like about the way they were managed. And an HR person would come in and sit in the corner and listen.

You can imagine such a meeting was uncomfortable for everybody—especially if you have a manager who isn't good at listening to begin with. Forcing the employees to go through these meetings felt punitive to the employees. So, what happened the following year? Not surprisingly, the employees decided together to give the manager high scores so they could avoid the useless but highly uncomfortable post-survey confrontational meetings. The bottom line: Be very careful that you allow and enable authentic, honest feedback.

Communication is one of the most pervasive challenges to developing a CX culture. When we are working with clients on customer journey maps, looking at processes, interviewing employees, and doing employee journey maps, we often find communication challenges.

Here are some tools to ensure your communication reinforces a customer-centric culture.

Invest in Customer Data Platforms

Customer data platforms are the way to share customer information. Review how you are presenting your internal communications about what you're doing with customers. Also, critically review your dashboards or other systems of reporting. You might find that you are never actually talking about customers! Instead, you are talking about results, sales . . . all kinds of things that aren't the customers.

CHAPTER 5

Look for ways to automate some of these communication pieces. Centralizing data into "one view" of the customer will help your employees serve them better. If centralizing all customer data is not yet an option, find workarounds and ensure your communication still serves the customer seamlessly. At all times you must continue to focus on sharing the customer's experience.

Your systems need to be aligned to your customer, not the other way around. With the right information, at the right time, for the right person, the customer will be served in a more personalized and successful way.

Given the cost of customer data platforms, it's important to make a long-term business case for these investments—a case that, as we said earlier, goes beyond just making customers happier. Senior leaders in your company need to see how not investing in customer data platforms and other systems can lead to lost sales, service costs, high return rates, and even employee turnover.

In addition to *communication*, investing in customer data platforms will add to your organization's *credibility*.

CX Storytelling

The TV show *Undercover Boss* shows organizational leaders disguising themselves to observe firsthand the customer journey in their organizations. Of course, engaging in such subterfuge is not realistic for every leader, manager, or technician. Without going "undercover," your leaders can still be involved by listening to real recordings from customer service calls, watching videos, or reading the thank-you messages directly. This is why storytelling is such an important skill for customer experience leaders. One of the great gifts that you can bring to your organizational culture is a selection of ways to share customer stories.

In addition to *communication*, storytelling will impact the *conscience* of your organization.

Feedback
Share feedback openly. Keep asking for and sharing both concerns *and* what's being done to address them.

You want to make sure that you have two-way communication when it comes to feedback. If you're a boomer, you might remember working on-site somewhere and having a break room in which the organization placed a suggestion box. The idea was that employees could make anonymous suggestions and talk about challenges without threat. Management would then look at those suggestions and make decisions. Today, suggestion boxes have been replaced by anonymous internal communication tools such as Slack, which you should encourage employees to use, or encourage them to leave a voicemail or send an email in an anonymous way.

If you have contact centers where people see how things are unfolding for the customer, give those people an easy process through which they can report the customer experience they are witnessing—a process (and this is important) that then closes the loop with them. If you ask people to make suggestions and they never hear anything back, you are not closing the communication loop. Show your teams that they are being heard and action is being taken. And if the suggestion cannot be implemented, explain why.

Listening to and acting on feedback is not just about *communication*; it's also vital to your *credibility*.

Answer Questions Publicly

Answer questions publicly; don't hide behind press releases or edited newsletters. When somebody submits an issue or even stops you in the hallway with a question or concern, remember that they might be representing many other people.

Derek Hall, the former CEO of the Arizona Diamondbacks, used to host a monthly chat with everybody interested in the organization. Think about the number and range of people involved with a major league baseball team. You have the fans, the workers selling hot dogs, and the management staff, not to mention the players and the coaches. Hall's philosophy was anything goes; ask anything. And he shared this anything-goes monthly chat far and wide—live-streaming it, for example—which the fans greatly appreciated. You can imagine how this initiative rebuilt the once-lost trust of fans and employees with the organization.

Think about how you can provide the same type of public forum for people to ask questions. And if someone asks you a question on the side, go ahead and share that question. You can say, "This is what we're hearing." That way people will know they're not alone. That transparency builds a culture of trust from the inside out.

Answering questions publicly is also about *credibility* as much as it is about *communication*.

Consistency
The third C is *consistency*. We've talked about consistency in previous chapters. To truly prove to others who you are, your behavior has to be consistent. This includes consistently showing up for your customers and consistently listening and responding to feedback from your employees.

Consistency will ensure that what happens inside the organization shows up on the outside. Daily employee experiences must be aligned with the company's customer experience mission to avoid developing a cynical culture that leads to poor results all around. Because an unhealthy culture can't hide from customers forever. I know of a B2B firm that actively promoted their friendly, open partnerships with clients—when, in fact, the firm's internal culture was one of one-upmanship and backstabbing. Needless to say, that firm is no longer in existence.

Focusing specifically on consistency between what's happening inside the organization and what's happening outside the organization is essential. If you're saying one thing publicly but behaving differently inside the organization, that inconsistency will create trust issues with your employees. They will realize the talk is just for investors or stakeholders but doesn't really reflect the walk for the customers. *Corporate hype* is communication about an organization that is spread through technology but dismissed by the employees as unrealistic hype. "That's just corporate hype," they say. "We're not even close to that."

Bottom line: Make sure you are consistently reflecting that customer experience mission, both inside and outside. Here are a few tools to ensure this consistency.

Undercover Boss (No Disguise Required)

Earlier, I mentioned the show *Undercover Boss*. To ensure consistency, forget the disguise and make every effort to interact directly with your customers. How many employees do you believe have interacted with a customer within the last thirty or sixty days?

Occasionally, CEOs of major corporations will announce formal plans to spend more time with frontline employees, interacting with customers. Imagine the impact on the organization's CX culture when it pays this kind of attention to the customer journey. By going in and working with their daily employees and interacting face-to-face with customers, these CEOs can come to really understand the reality of their customer journey. They can see whether or not employees are walking the CX walk both inside and outside the organization.

Improving your *consistency* by interacting with customers also increases your *credibility*.

Inviting Customers into the Process

Inviting customers into the process is another important step to ensure consistency between the inside and outside of the organization. There are various ways to accomplish this, including establishing a customer advisory board or conducting customer interviews, which can be done formally or informally. If your next customer advisory board session or focus group isn't scheduled for months and you feel out of touch, invite a few customers in to see what the organization is doing next or to try out a new idea.

Collecting spontaneous feedback will tell you quite a bit about consistency. If customers tell you something is working or isn't, and you're seeing the same thing in your organization, you know where to prioritize. But if what's not working on the outside is not internally apparent, then you have a misalignment point to address. Interviewing both employees and customers is key to finding such areas of misalignment.

Inviting customers into the process is another way improving your *consistency* strengthens your *credibility*.

CX Strategic Council

A CX strategic council is a cross-functional team that can change the game. Note that what I call a strategic council may be called something else in your organization. You might call it simply your CX team. Sometimes this type of strategic council is called a governance board. Whatever you call it, the goal is to centralize how your CX efforts are prioritized and resourced. The CX strategic council is the team that makes decisions around customer experience priorities.

The cross-functional nature of such a team is key because cross-functional team members will better understand the customer experience and the efforts involved in terms of their specific functions. This type of strategic council can thus spread the CX culture throughout the organization almost by osmosis.

To further improve the effectiveness of such a council, define the roles and responsibilities of each council member, the goals of the team, and the rubric for evaluating customer experience efforts. Also make sure the CX strategic council meets regularly, perhaps monthly, to review customer feedback, new insights, and recommendations for improvement. Through the CX strategic council, the chief experience officer (CXO), chief customer officer (CCO), or other C-suite leaders can sponsor and approve funding for the recommendations that emerge from the council's meeting. The council helps every leader in the organization have the right customer information to make better decisions.

In addition to ensuring *consistency*, a strategic council facilitates *communication* and strengthens your *credibility*.

Bring the Entire Team Onstage

We've talked about the C-suite and how important they are, but if they're the only ones getting the attention, if everybody's just raving about the CMO and her marketing team, it's very easy for people to feel unheard. In your role as a CX leader, look for opportunities to bring the folks onstage who make a difference in the customer experience.

Say you asked for an improvement in the product; the improvement came through, and your results went up. Talk about the team in the background, the engineers who actually designed the improvement. Acknowledge how they contributed to delivering for your customers.

How do you find the people who are contributing? Look for the changes being made that truly make a difference and find out who is involved. Because if you talk about only the customer-facing folks or only the leaders, you're missing a whole bunch of people who are part of that process.

Bringing the entire team onstage not only ensures *consistency* but also, as with many tools in the consistency toolbox, improves your *communication* and your *credibility*.

Credibility

The fourth and final C is *credibility*. This is where the rubber meets the road. It's not enough to tell people to "think of the customer." If you talk about customer experience but never take action, never show results, and never get other folks involved, it's a losing mission. Because after a while, your employees will look around, see the inconsistency, see the lack of action, and disengage.

Credibility means stating explicitly, "This is the goal, and this is what we're doing about it," and then reporting back on how the goal was met or why it wasn't. Talk is

CHAPTER 5

cheap. Credibility demands that employees incorporate the customer experience mission into actionable ideas. There are a number of different ways to do this.

First, think about adding a customer experience mission question to each agenda. You could print out the whole mission statement and then compare results to the mission. For example, if you're meeting about accuracy rate, discuss how the accuracy rate matters for the mission, then look at the numbers and, perhaps, explain how the numbers need to increase to reflect the mission goal. These types of discussions will increase the credibility of the CX mission.

Incorporate customer feedback, data, and quotes into project plans and product road maps whenever you can. Again, you want the customer to be in the center. If you're talking about whatsits and how to produce them, but you're not talking about how your customers use those whatsits or what they need from those whatsits or things that they've asked for that your organization hasn't yet delivered on, then the CX mission can be quickly overlooked.

Your customers are not going to be happy if you just keep doing the same thing without including them in the process. Feedback from customers will provide incentives to employees to develop customer-centric ideas, thus contributing to the mission.

Rewarding employees who earn high marks from customers will also incentivize customer-centric ideas. Find a way to leverage that success to inspire others. This means looking at why particular employees are getting great marks from customers. What can others learn from them?

Forrester, in their 2023 State of Customer Obsession survey, revealed that 100 percent of customer-obsessed companies prioritized teaching employees how to play their part.[2] This statistic underscores the importance of educating employees about their role in driving the business forward with a customer-first approach.

How can you motivate and reward employees to enhance your CX credibility? Don't hesitate to celebrate. In any extraordinary culture, you will see successes being celebrated again and again. Zappos is known for having in-office parades. Rackspace rewards great customer service reps with a straitjacket to recognize their fanatical customer support.

Celebrating success not only ensures *credibility* but also adds to the collective *conscience* of your organization and improves your *communication*.

CX Maturity

Another way of thinking about this process is through the metaphor of maturity—growing up as a CX culture. That transformative process can be broken down into five stages: awareness, adoption, alignment, accountability, and advocacy.

CHAPTER 5

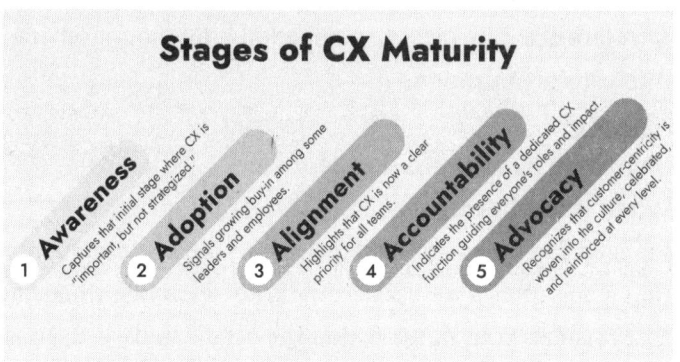

One Approach to CX Maturity

Mission Moments

One way to check in and confirm that your organization is following the four C's and living the mission is through what I call *mission moments*. These are moments where you can see the mission reflected... or not. You have to be honest and accept the hard truths about how you are living up to the mission, on the one hand, and what you may need to change, on the other. For example, is there a process that is preventing employees from living up to that mission? Examine stories of customer interactions and feedback. And don't ignore employee interactions. The alignment between the customer experience and employee experience is very important. Mission moments provide the opportunity for you to talk about your CX goals as a community.

Here are four ideas for embedding mission moments into your organization.

Share and Ask for Mission Moments When Interviewing

Job candidates should know if their values are well aligned with the organization. If you ask the candidate to describe a moment that matches your mission, and the candidate is struggling with a response, that tells you something about either the candidate or your mission—because perhaps you need to refine it.

On the other hand, the candidate might say, "Oh my gosh, I love that because..." and then tell you about something they did in the past. The job interview can be a powerful way to use mission moments.

Create a Habit in the First Ninety Days

This mission moment idea involves the employee onboarding process. The best employee journeys start with a focus on the customer experience. You want to make sure that by the end of ninety days, they not only know the mission but also know this is how you live it and that this is important. They understand that you are going to incorporate the mission into everything you do.

It's possible that if you are introducing a mission and you already have a really well-established team, you might think that introducing the mission to new employees doesn't need to be done immediately. Fight that impulse. Not only is it better for new employees to understand the importance of the CX mission immediately, but you are also losing a communication opportunity, because new hires can help you spread the word.

Start Key Meetings with a Mission Moment
I recommend this for every organization. Start key meetings with a clear reminder to all of who you are as an organization. You can do this at the beginning of the meeting through stories of moments when employees and the organization overall lived up to the mission—or when they didn't. It's very important to have that less pleasant conversation as well.

Ask a different team member to bring a mission moment to each meeting. These can be stories of moments employees and the organization overall lived up to the CX mission, or when they didn't. Both positive and negative mission moments offer chances to learn and improve. One organization focused on empowering leaders, so they often had lessons learned by discussing when they *failed* to deliver on that mission. With each story, a culture of honesty and accountability was reinforced.

You could also put the mission moment at the end of the meeting. People can call each other out and say something like, "I just want to recognize how great it was that Jillian was able to deliver on the mission in this way." The mission moment is a powerful way to level up your CX meetings and connect the team not only to the mission but to one another as well.

Mission Moments: The Game

A mission moment game supports the concept of the CX Mission Statement as a change management and communication tool. To gamify mission moments, award points when new employees either witness others living up to the mission or when they themselves see an opportunity to do so. This can be handled with a simple form that asks:

1. What mission moment did you witness or deliver?
2. Why do you think it lived up to your organization's mission or not?
3. Is there an employee or team to celebrate for living up to the mission?
4. Is there a lesson or idea to improve things for the future?

Through mission moments, we reinforce the idea that the CX mission is not just something we're talking about; it's something we're living. Mission moments also indicate potential improvement areas, as when people might say, "I couldn't live up to the mission because of this" or "I witnessed somebody creating a clever workaround on one of our processes to deliver on the mission."

Sometimes our processes, our technology, our tools, our employee training, and so forth get in the way of delivering on the mission. Ensuring that your people have their radar up, so to speak, for those mission moments, and stay honest about whether they or others are delivering on the mission will reveal a whole set of areas to improve for customer experience. Mission moments also take the critique out of the realm of individuals and help you objectively explore why the organization was or wasn't able to live up to the mission. Asking what happened that allowed us (or didn't allow us) to live up to the mission in a specific instance leads to rich conversations about process, tools, employee interactions, and more.

Those behind-the-scenes situations are exactly what lead to experiences for customers. Yet often we talk about those things as if they are separate from customer experience. Mission moments lead to deeper understanding and a willingness to explore what's working and what's not.

Mission moments bring it all together. In addition to enhancing *credibility*, mission moments will raise the collective *conscience* of your organization and improve *communication* and CX *consistency*.

What About a Toxic Culture?

We've been discussing how to create a customer-first culture. But what if you have a culture in place that is so toxic there is no chance for such a change to materialize?

Some organizations might start with a "sales" culture. Competitive monthly and quarterly benchmarks for sales lead to aggressive sales tactics. Top leaders declaring that the organization will now embody a customer-centric attitude won't magically change those behaviors. Salespeople will probably still believe they are judged on their numbers, even if they aren't anymore. And if the numbers aren't good, they are going to start pointing fingers at other departments.

That's how you know you've got trouble. One of the biggest flags for a toxic culture is the blame game. "We can't deliver on a great customer experience because of so-and-so or so-and-so department." If that's the case in your organization, getting out of the blame game is a top priority.

Help everyone in the organization realize that you are all in this to deliver for the customer. People mess up, departments mess up, deadlines are missed—that's all part of the human experience. In response to these types of issues, focus on understanding why something happened rather than who did it. Look at root cause analysis. Try to understand what you can do next time to avoid the same problem.

If you're not in a top leadership position, perhaps there is less you can do about a toxic culture. But you can play your part in turning down the volume on the blame game and focus more on what all of you can do better next time. At the very least, make sure that *you* are not adding to a toxic culture, because that will not serve your customers, your employees, or your CX mission goals.

The Four C's Scorecard

Here's a scorecard to help you gauge the performance of your organization on the four C's. Sitting down and thinking about what score you should get can be very enlightening. It can also help you figure out where you might need to focus, where you might be totally missing the boat, and what you can do about it.

Final Thoughts

Creating or contributing to a customer-first culture is not easy. This is not about getting one process right. This is about building and nurturing space for each individual in your organization to be who they are within the context of a collective culture.

That's no small feat. One place to start is to get to know your HR folks, your training people, and your onboarding people, because they are often the people who start building the culture throughout. Invite them to join the CX team or ask for their feedback. Culture change begins with small steps and cross-functional relationships. Cultures are never built in a day. They are developed over time and evolve. The four C's offer a blueprint for creating a customer-first culture that creates great experiences for your customers—in, large part by paying equal attention to the employee experience.

Four C's of Culture Scorecard

Mark your score from 1 to 5 for each C.
Then, add your score from each C row on the next page to find your total score.

Four C's of Culture	1	2	3	4	5
Conscience	You have a CX Mission Statement, but it is not socialized often. You don't have a recent Customer Journey Map (CJM) or refer to the customer's wants and needs.				Your employees know the CX Mission Statement and live it because they understand their impact on the customer experience. Your customer's needs and feelings are understood at all levels.
Communication	Your leaders don't communicate about your CX mission. Frontline employees don't feel heard, or worse, they have stopped giving suggestions.				Your leaders communicate about the CX mission often through various channels. Your frontline customers feel comfortable giving feedback or submitting ideas for improvement.
Consistency	Employees feel the disconnect between how customers and employees are treated.				Employees exemplify the CX Mission Statement externally because it is modeled internally.
Credibility	The CX mission is a poster on a wall or a line in an email signature, but it doesn't impact customer interactions.				Employees understand the CX Mission and are recognized for living the CX Mission. Customer feedback is disseminated and utilized for decision-making and prioritization.

Total Score: ____ + _____ + ____ + ____ = _____
  Conscience Communication Consistency Credibility

CHAPTER 6

Four C's of Culture Results

If you scored:

5 – 10	It's time to focus on your CX culture. Pick one C and determine your next steps to enhance your CX culture this month.
11 – 15	You have a solid foundation for your CX culture, but there is room for improvement. What is something you can accomplish this quarter to advance your culture?
16 – 20	Congratulations! You've clearly put in effort to create and maintain a CX culture. Culture is always evolving so get ahead by determining the next step you can take in the next six months.

CHAPTER 6

BUILDING NEW HABITS... AS A TEAM

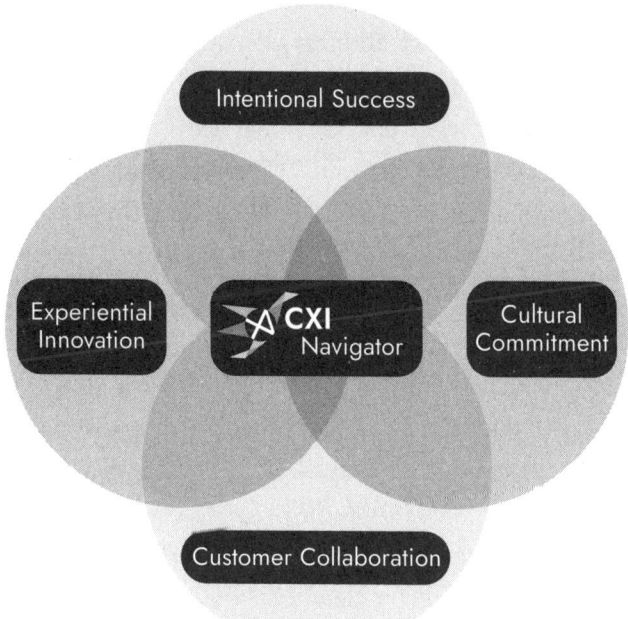

CXI Navigator Framework

I've been challenged when I discuss customer experience as a business discipline. The same people who challenge these ideas as "common sense" or simple "soft skills" can't necessarily grasp that to deliver exceptional, intentional, proactive customer experiences, we must first determine what we are actually going to do and then approach that commitment with discipline. That means creating habits, goals, metrics, and more. That means actually acting... every day.

Let's put ourselves back into thinking that CX is a nice-to-have but not a must-have for a thriving business. If we're thinking like that, it's easy to imagine that we can sprinkle that fairy dust around and just ask people to "get it."

Nope. Creating real, tangible business discipline around customer experience efforts is what leads to real results.

What is business discipline? Consider a sales team. They are often held accountable for the actions they take that lead to sales, not just for the sales themselves. That means they might track how many clients they reach out to, what trade events they attend, how many leads are created, and so on. When we skip this part of the customer experience strategy in our organizations, we bank on hope. And, as we know, hope is not a strategy.

Intentional Success

We know that having a clear CX Mission Statement and CX Success Blueprint can help you determine what is most important. Take a look at your goals. Break down what needs to happen to achieve them.

CHAPTER 6

For example, if you have a stated goal in your success blueprint regarding more customer outreach to improve retention rates, then create monthly, weekly, and daily goals around that. How might customers require outreach? When? What should you be reporting on in any given structure? There are often assumptions, unspoken frustrations, and even myths that are followed instead of approaching this part of the business as ... well ... part of the business.

If you've been assigned the general task of "leading CX" or "improving our customer experience," you might relate to this story.

One of our clients at Experience Investigators came to us with a customer experience team. Their head of NPS came for coaching as she was frustrated; she felt she was doing the right things and not getting the traction she wanted. However, they were literally called the NPS Team. They were charged with improving net promoter score

(NPS). Their role was really just reporting on the scores and trying to get others to care about them.

There are so many issues with this. First, this team had no accountability and had frankly lost the plot. NPS is not an outcome. It's a measurement. It's one measurement that helps us know what customers have said. It doesn't show us how customers have behaved or how this relates to our organizational goals. As CX leaders, that's our job.

This is the discipline we need to bring to the CX conversation: the daily discipline of asking what we can do to achieve our CX goals. We do this by evaluating data, sharing insights, and gaining buy-in throughout the organization. That's no small task. In the case of our client, it was an evolution, not a revolution.

We determined that there had been too much emphasis on reporting NPS and not enough on what efforts were needed to actually improve that score. The team had been meeting with various business units, asking them to improve their scores. But the business units weren't given tools or information beyond the customer feedback. It's simply not fair to ask typically overwhelmed leaders to "do something" without providing the right information, specific goals, or the tools to actually take action. We found that many customer comments discussed slow response times. So, we helped our client focus on one big effort around responsiveness. This allowed the NPS Team to focus on a specific and important goal. Instead of just mentioning "responsiveness," we created specific goals for each business unit. These goals were measured and reported on monthly, and the team gave ideas and feedback on how to continuously improve them.

That became the rallying cry for the business units: How can we speed up our responsiveness?

Business discipline regarding strategic goals requires a clear definition and understanding of the goals you have—outside of your feedback metrics.

Oh, and the NPS Team? They're now called the Customer Experience Team. They added staff members and created better understanding throughout the organization. It took several months and certainly wasn't an overnight success. But it was a success nonetheless. And that was all because they had the right mindset, strategy, and discipline to get there.

Cultural Commitment

Discipline is required to get into new habits. That means a goal like "leverage mission moments more" has to be clearly defined and understood. In one case, this meant bringing in the internal communication team for a large organization. They needed to help get the word out about the CX Mission Statement, what it was, what it stood for, and what to do with it. With their help, we created a mission moment contest on the corporate intranet. Now if this was just launched and touted once or twice, it wouldn't have had any traction. Instead, there was real discipline around delivering updates, recognizing and rewarding winners, and creating a true culture of customer-centric coworkers.

Some of the most straightforward discipline is typically applied in the customer collaboration realm.

There are many organizations that start their customer experience journey by tackling customer feedback as an entire strategy. We've talked about why this is a flawed

CHAPTER 6

approach on its own, but overall, this is a key part of any customer experience strategy. The business discipline here is around having a centralized, integrated feedback strategy. How are you collecting feedback? How are you evaluating it? What are you doing to close the loop with customers and employees? Are you asking too few or too many questions? Are you leveraging AI and other tools to expedite action? There are many points of business discipline I bet you're already including in your customer experience strategy. The key is to make sure that the feedback you're collecting is delivering the right insights to help you take action in ways that align with your overall definition of success.

Experiential Innovation

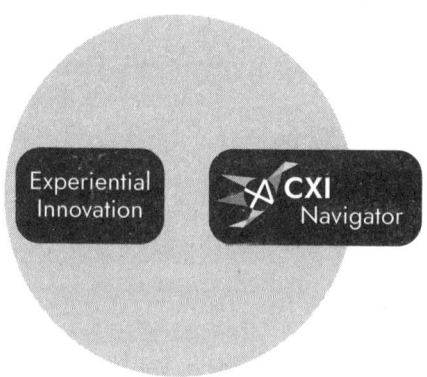

This is where customer experience strategy becomes a game changer when leveraged with the right business discipline.

This is how your effort to create meaningful moments for customers becomes a competitive advantage. Yet this is often overlooked.

Innovation doesn't just happen. While we love stories in which accidental innovation happens (like the Post-it), in reality we need to be intentional about innovation too.

How? By creating a regular rhythm of innovation. One way we do this is through quarterly or semi-annual Disruptor Days. In these workshops, we invite lots of cross-functional teams to consider what the customer journey *could* be if we were free of limitations. We do this by using customer journey mapping as a tool to look at the potential ideal customer experience. We call it Disruptor Day because we want lots of disruption. We want big ideas that maybe a start-up in our industry would consider if reimagining the entire customer journey.

Some ideas are wackier than others—and that's okay! But a list of twenty crazy ideas usually contains two or three potential ways to make things better for customers over time and even more that can improve the experience just a little in the short term. Innovation comes in big and small ways. By applying the discipline to carve out time for a Disruptor Day every quarter or twice a year, you are putting in the effort that leads to the solutions you're seeking.

Discipline is about ownership. We need to own the outcome, which means having the right mindset, defining the correct strategy, and applying the right discipline to our daily efforts.

CHAPTER 6

See how this all fits together? ☺

The Customer Experience Charter: Getting Things Done!

There's one more thing you need to achieve intentional success, cultural commitment, customer collaboration, and experiential innovation. You need more than one CX change agent with a dream. You need a team.

Have you ever been on a team that includes members from all over the organization? Maybe a planning committee or special project team? If so, you can probably relate to how this often means people joining up and then becoming too busy, too distracted, or simply not caring enough to make it all the way to the completion of the project.

I remember sitting on a team like this for a large client that was launching a new digital tool. This was a *huge* undertaking, and there was a nonnegotiable deadline. That first meeting had so many people! There were representatives from technology, marketing, sales, product, legal . . . it was standing room only in the biggest conference room they had! Everyone seemed to want to be part of this new and exciting endeavor.

But after that first meeting, the regular meetings became smaller. Fewer people could make the time for them, and there was confusion when some leaders sent people in their place. The new person would walk into that third or fifth or seventh meeting and announce that they had no background in what was happening. So time was spent getting those short-timers up to speed instead of making real progress.

I've seen this happen with CX teams too. It can seem exciting and new at first, but then you're left with team members who are checked out. Yet again, customer experience is treated as something to talk about but not really be accountable for.

Enter the Customer Experience Charter.

The CX Charter is a brief document that captures the goals and priorities of the CX leadership team and the processes and agreements for achieving those goals and priorities. The charter creates a written package that can be communicated to the rest of the organization, especially to those leaders and teams you need to include in some way.

The CX Charter is an idea taken from the best practices of project management. If you've ever been involved with a high-stakes project with a good project manager, you probably found that they were guided by a project charter.

Part of the function of the charter is documentation—making sure everything is documented so that everybody is on the same page. Another major function is prioritizing. With customer experience, everything can feel like a priority—from customer feedback to input from corporate leaders to aligning customer experience with organizational goals. Having a CX Charter along with those first two tools in your tool kit, the CX Mission Statement and the CX

CHAPTER 6

Success Blueprint, will help you define your priorities in a very powerful way.

A charter will also help pull together the right team and keep them motivated and productive. Leading a CX program calls for a cross-functional team. This team can include CX leaders like you but can also involve people who are not necessarily invested in the idea of customer experience yet. It can even include people who will be involved for only a short time, depending on the specific initiative. Initiatives might be working with digital specialists to improve a digital part of the experience or working with the learning and development team to create CX knowledge and training for new employees.

But make no mistake: If your actions and priorities are not well documented, a CX team that begins a project with momentum and enthusiasm may soon find engagement waning. If people attend a meeting and it's not well organized, or they're not exactly sure what the outcomes are supposed to be, they might simply decide not to show up for the next one.

With a charter, you can quickly get somebody up to speed about who you are, what's important to you, what their role might be, and what you expect from them. And if you are just starting to build a team, your charter document will reveal in some detail how a cross-functional CX team can help you achieve your desired outcomes.

Let's do some recruiting! Who are you targeting for participation in the CX leadership team?

Who Should Be on the Team?

Much of this depends on what you're tasked to do. I suggest beginning with a brainstorming session. In this session, you might first identify people who belong to teams that would have some influence over what you are trying to accomplish. You might also identify people who are accountable for the different parts of the organization that will be involved in your CX initiatives. You could also approach building your team from a less utilitarian perspective—for example, identifying the people you just want to be involved because you know they're going to be truly committed to the CX goals and will help spread the word throughout the organization.

Another approach to building your team is to examine your list of priorities and think about the output you are looking for—for example, which parts of the journey you want to fix first, or perhaps what new elements can be introduced to it. For example, one year you might decide to prioritize innovation. Once that decision is made, you can think about who needs to be involved.

You also want team members who are close to the customer experience. With a number of CX leadership teams, I've seen the frontline workers—the people who are interacting with customers every day—being ignored or kept out of the loop. What happens if, when you make a big change, you don't include the people who are answering calls and responding to inquiries? Those people will find themselves in a position in which they don't have the right information

CHAPTER 6

to do their jobs and are more likely to disappoint a customer who knows more than they do.

So if you're in product, you might want to include the digital experience team or your customer service folks. If you have a front line with cashiers or service reps or agents dealing directly with customers, you will want to include them in this cross-functional team. You might want to include people in your supply chain or team members who are involved with CX governance.

Another set of people who need to be involved will come from your organization's top leadership. When you have big goals, you will need some sponsorship from either the C-suite or your executive or your boss's boss—however the hierarchy is structured in the organization. The bottom line is that you need somebody who has more authority and accountability, especially around budget and resources, to be aware of the team and its goals. Think about who can sponsor your efforts.

Once you have in mind all the people from throughout the organization who will contribute to your CX efforts, you will be able to develop or adjust your CX Charter to better fit their needs and interests, increasing your chances of recruitment.

Now, as the final touch to your CX training, let's put that CX Charter together and get you moving.

CHAPTER 7

A CX CHARTER OF YOUR OWN

READY TO DEVELOP YOUR OWN CX CHARTER? YOU WANT TO create one that provides the following information:

CX Mission Statement. This is your North Star. You want to ensure you are interacting with and living up to your mission. The mission must guide everything you do.

CX Goals. The only way to know where you're going is to know your goals. The CX Success Blueprint can help you define your goals so that everybody is aligned on the same priorities.

CX Roles. Who's doing what, why, how, and when? Identify the sponsor. Who is going to own the project? You need someone who's accountable for each of the improvements you want to make. This is important! This is how you add accountability to each role.

CX Priorities. Which efforts should be prioritized, and which efforts have limitations that make them less of a priority? A priority matrix charting the feasibility and impact of individual efforts is a powerful guide for prioritization.

CX Communication. How will you communicate and socialize your efforts and results among the people who need to know what's going on? These include your leaders and the frontline people I talked about earlier—those who are interacting with the customers. What do they need to know about these improvements? What can you share organizationally that will help everybody understand the customer experience journey and how important it is?

CX Management. Customer experience does not happen without leadership and CX management. How do you get all this done? Who's accountable for what, and how do you put it into a structure that makes sense for how you work together?

Let's explore these six elements in more detail.

CX Mission Statement

The CX Mission Statement, of course, is your North Star. In your CX Charter, you want the mission statement front and center. For anyone included in your CX work, the mission is the starting point. It is the mission statement that will help everybody understand how you want the organization to show up for your customers.

A major challenge with describing the mission is that people tend to think in terms of products and services. But mission isn't really about the product or service—it's about what those products and services can do for your customers. For example, you're not just selling a ticket to a sporting event; you're selling an experience that they will remember forever. You're selling something that is about their legacy with their family. Make sure your people are thinking beyond the literal product and service when you talk about your mission.

One of my favorite stories about understanding a mission involves the US efforts in the 1960s to put a man on the moon—which at the time seemed like a long-shot goal to everybody. As the story goes, President Kennedy was walking through NASA in 1962, looking at all the rockets, and saw a janitor sweeping up. The president asked him what he did at NASA. The janitor replied, "I'm helping put a man on the moon." He knew that was his mission.

That is the spirit of the CX Mission Statement. It is about what you're trying to do. It is your purpose. And it unites everyone around how the organization delivers for customers. If you want to explore their understanding of the mission, ask your people, "What is most important about the experience we deliver?" If they can't answer that question, they may not be connected with the mission, and achieving the goals listed in the CX chart will be that much harder.

CX Goals

Your CX goals are the focus of the CX Success Blueprint, which we discussed in chapter 3. Remember, however, that the blueprint is about specific outcomes for the *organization* achieved through CX goals—how customer retention helps the organization, for example. CX goals are goals that help your organization become as successful as possible. Look at the specific objectives and make sure they tie back to your CX efforts, organizational goals, and leadership goals.

One way to assess the quality and effectiveness of your goals is to use the SMIRC goal-setting framework. SMIRC stands for social, measurable, inspiring, relevant, and contextual. *Social* goals are goals that cut across departments and align with overall organizational goals. *Measurable* goals can be quantified based on reliably measurable data. *Inspiring* goals tell a meaningful story or are based on a customer's "before" and ideal "after" states. *Relevant* goals take into consideration the unique obstacles, conditions, and desired outcomes of your target customers but also the unique obstacles, conditions, and opportunities related to your organization. And finally, *contextual* goals are goals that fit within or align with the context of the customer, the organization's leadership, and the other participants in the CX initiative.

The SMIRC framework enables you to think about your goals in a broader sense. You face a number of challenges as CX leaders. Not everybody understands CX or understands your role within your organization. Using the SMIRC criteria for your goals will help clarify why CX is important.

CX Roles

I covered the challenge of recruiting the right people for your team. But identifying the right people is only the first challenge; the second is to encourage them to become

CHAPTER 7

involved. This does not mean you have the power to pluck people away from their jobs. You will not be changing their job title or becoming their boss. Instead, you will give them enough sense of responsibility and ownership and inspiration that they will want to help meet the CX goals you've outlined in the charter because it's going to be a win for them as well.

Once you have the team chosen, you want to clearly define their responsibilities and deliverables. The information and responsibilities sheet shown on the following page will help. This sheet lists the strategies, actions, and specific outcomes for which each member is responsible. I would also recommend adding how outcomes will be measured, when and for how long these outcomes will be measured, and how frequently this member will check in with the CX team.

This last item—how frequently a team member will check in with the CX team—might seem very logistical, but it is important.

The more detailed you can be about your charter, the better. In addition to tracking who's meeting and when, and who's responsible for what, set some ground rules about meeting attendance as well. Perhaps a CX team member can send somebody else from their team or send something through email in advance. The more specific you are about the expectations of each team member, the more successful the team will be.

CX Team Member #1 — Information and Responsibilities

Fill in the blanks:

Name: _____

Role: _____

Strategies this member is responsible for: _____
_____
_____

Actions this member is responsible for: _____
_____
_____

Specific outcomes this member is responsible for: _____
_____
_____

How outcomes will be measured: _____
_____
_____

When and for how long these outcomes will be measured:
_____
_____

How frequently this member will check in with the CX Team:
_____
_____

CX Team Member: Information and Responsibilities

CHAPTER 7

Note that the strategies or outcomes for which an individual team member is responsible do not necessarily have to be plural. Sometimes a team member will be responsible for one specific item or initiative because their part of the customer journey is very specific.

I worked on one project in which customer journey mapping revealed a huge problem around invoicing. Customers hated the system. They would call in continuously with complaints, and their dissatisfaction created all kinds of service costs—the company often had to resend invoices, and there was a big gap in payment. For decades (no exaggeration!) invoicing was a massive pain point for both the organization and their customers, yet no one had thought to look at the source of the problems. Instead, the invoicing team was responsible for fixing the individual problems as they occurred. Nobody liked that, neither the customers nor the invoicing team. But it had been done that way for so long that nobody thought about it as a customer experience pain point.

Once the CX team started to come together, they realized something had to be done about invoicing. For the first time, a member from the invoicing team was invited to join the CX team. That person's help, support, and specific input created a transformational change in the organization's invoicing—a transformation achieved because, finally, a person from the invoicing team had been given a clear role, with responsibility and target outcomes, in the organization's CX efforts.

CX Priorities

Setting CX priorities is the pain point of many CX teams. The reason is that the people on a cross-functional team will inevitably have different priorities.

If you have, for instance, somebody from your marketing team as part of your CX team, they will undoubtedly apply a marketing lens to whatever the topic might be. If a list of improvements is on the table, they will be pushing for improvements that address marketing concerns first. At the same time, the team member from sales will be advocating for a focus on sales-related items.

As the CX team leader, it is your job to help manage sometimes conflicting priorities.

One path to prioritizing items on your list of potential actions is to ask: What larger goals are these priorities tied to? Your CX Success Blueprint can be very helpful here. Your CX Success Blueprint might have designated "increase retention" as a key goal for the organization. You can now look at the potential action items and decide which is more likely to help your organization increase retention the most.

Focusing the team on the larger goals of the organization is one important way to build a consensus on priorities. At the same time, you want to emphasize that other priorities are also important. Unfortunately, you all have only so much time, so many people, and so many resources at your disposal. You must show the team that attempting to tackle everything and thus getting spread too thin is not the way to make any change. You prioritize

CHAPTER 7

based on your organizational goals and your mission, you accomplish that top priority, and then you move on to the next.

Thus, when someone comes to you and says that the organization's signage is not great, you can agree...but then respond, "Let me show you what we've agreed are the goals. You see, signage will not significantly change the metrics that we are tracking or drive us closer to our organizational goals."

At the other end, you want to be realistic about your limitations. If your legacy computing system is old and cranky, but you know the organization is not going to improve it for two years, there is very little you can do. The organization's leaders have their priorities elsewhere, and you must work within that constraint.

The simple tool we introduced earlier, called a priority matrix, and also shown on the next page, can be applied here as well. It will help you set priorities based on what you can realistically achieve and what will have the most influence over the goals and outcomes you want to achieve. The priority matrix will help you think through which actions you should prioritize by focusing on two key questions:

1. What impact will this action have on our business outcomes? In other words, is this action worth the investment?
2. How feasible is this? Is it an action you can accomplish quickly, or could it turn into a long-term diversion? Adding a thank-you to your invoices is a lot different than saying you need to totally upgrade

your invoicing system. Sometimes it's a huge thing; sometimes it's a quick win.

The priority matrix is also valuable because it gives you the opportunity to record potential actions. What are the things that you want to do? What would that look like?

Priority Matrix *Fill in the squares:*

High Impact / Low Feasibility	High Impact / High Feasibility
Low Impact / Low Feasibility	Low Impact / High Feasibility

Priority Matrix

Let's take a close look at each of the four quadrants in the priority matrix.

CHAPTER 7

High Impact / Low Feasibility
In the upper-left quadrant is high impact / low feasibility. This quadrant is for items that are going to have a major impact but will be hard to implement. Changing the whole invoice system would go in this quadrant. It's not going to be feasible for a little while, but you know it's going to have a big impact.

High Impact / High Feasibility
The upper-right quadrant is for the quick wins. These are the things you want to execute as soon as you possibly can because they will have an impact. Whether it's something you could do tomorrow, within a month, or even within a year, you know that it can be implemented. This quadrant is where you start your prioritization.

Low Impact / Low Feasibility
The lower-left quadrant is low impact / low feasibility. These are items that are probably not going to move any needles. But not only are they not going to drive the goals you are trying to achieve—they also are going to be hard to do. You might have a list here that you can *almost* ignore. I say almost because, every once in a while, something in this quadrant might get promoted for one reason or another. But for now, you can put the items in this quadrant aside.

Low Impact / High Feasibility
The lower-right quadrant is low impact / high feasibility—initiatives you could execute without too many resources

but that are not going to have the impact you want. Some people might argue that since you can do it, go ahead and do it. It's true that sometimes little things do add up, but a quadrant like this also helps you determine what is really a priority and what is not.

Fill out this matrix as a team. As you do, two or three items will start to be recognized as the highest priorities. If there are no clear-cut winners, then put the priorities to a vote. What I like to do with CX teams is print the items out separately, put them around the room, and ask the team members to use Post-it notes to vote for which ones they would prioritize. Each team member might get two votes, for example, depending on how many options you have. Inevitably, the top priorities will start to emerge. This method will ensure that you have buy-in from the cross-functional team.

CX Communication

There are three important questions to answer in developing your communication. The first: What is your communication *strategy*? It's vital to make sure the whole organization knows about what you are doing as a team. This communication strategy can cover anything from the insights that you are uncovering from customer feedback to what actions you are taking to what successful outcomes you have been able to achieve already.

Communicating your successes not only highlights positive outcomes but also provides an opportunity to recognize

CHAPTER 7

those teams who maybe aren't officially in the customer experience sphere but have helped you with an important project to improve the customer journey. The resulting message is clear: Customer experience is an organization-wide initiative involving people from across the organization.

The second question related to communications is who is *responsible* for it. Which of your team members has the specific responsibility of ensuring that news about the initiatives and accomplishments of your CX team is spread throughout the organization? Notable in this responsibility is making sure that the leadership in your company is aware of the changes you're making and the ways that you are driving strategy.

Third question: What is the ongoing *cadence* of communication? It's important to communicate on a regular basis—in fact, ensuring the regularity of communication is the greatest responsibility of your communication point person. The cadence of communication is an important decision. Too much communication—we all know the frustration of multiple emails a day from the same sender—can be counterproductive. At the same time, the CX team must not be forgotten. So perhaps your cadence can be as simple as sending an email every month about what you're doing in customer experience.

On the following page, you will find a tool called a Communication Channels Chart. This is useful, especially in large organizations that have many different ways to communicate. From an internal newsletter or an intranet to a Slack channel or a town hall meeting, there are multiple channels through which you can communicate. Brainstorm about what's available to you, how often you can realistically communicate through a channel, and with which channel owners you want to build a relationship.

Communication Channels Chart

List = all communication channels your organization uses as well as how often communications are issued.

Channel	Frequency	Owner
Example: Company newsletter	Monthly	Susan in HR

Communication Channels Chart

This tool, if you revisit it consistently during your regular meetings, can help you keep track of what's happening along the potentially many communication channels in your organization. It can also help you identify and follow up on new communication opportunities. In large organizations, people may not know about all the communication channels available to them or the new channels coming online. Use this chart to keep track.

CX Management

A key element in the CX Charter will be specifics on how to make all of this—putting together the CX Mission Statement, developing the CX Success Blueprint, and everything else that we have covered in this book—actually work. There's a tendency, unfortunately, to overlook the management of the process. And when dealing with cross-functional teams especially, failing to address how the process will be managed can often lead to eventual failure.

I've seen a number of cross-functional teams that start strong and fizzle out. In the beginning, team members show up with a positive collaborative mindset, and everybody's working together well. Over time, however, the questions start: What are we doing this time? What's the agenda? Who's doing what? Without a specific management structure in place, the ad hoc early progress built on enthusiasm is bound to run out of steam.

Don't leave momentum and motivation to chance. At the beginning, establish specifics on how people will work together—as I put it, how they will *show up* for each other. For example, if a team member can't make a meeting, they need to send somebody in their place or submit their update through email or find another solution. The point is that expectations for team members are established from the start.

Management also includes managing meetings, which are the drivers of the process in most organizations. In the charter, people should find the answers to detailed meeting questions such as, How often are we going to meet? Who needs to be at which meetings? What times are we going to meet? What are the expectations for actions and communication about actions between the meetings?

It's probably clear by now that you will need a project manager to guide the process. This project manager should understand not only how to delegate but also how to follow up. They must make sure that people have something to do, understand what they are doing, and are getting their tasks done.

To give you an idea of why designating a project manager is important, here is just a partial list of that manager's responsibilities:

- Identify who's showing up and participating—and who's less committed.
- Outline expectations before meetings, including setting the agenda and identifying what each team member should be prepared to deliver.
- Encourage team members to put meetings on their calendars and set the expectation that absences are to be minimized.

CHAPTER 7

- Document accountabilities emerging from each meeting, follow up with attendees to ensure clarity on their accountabilities, and check in on progress between meetings.
- If tasks or initiatives fall behind, get more team members involved to pick up the slack.

This is standard project management, and no matter how creative or motivated or enthusiastic the CX team might be, you need that project management structure, including the project manager, in place.

Remember that the CX Charter is a relatively brief document. You want to have clear answers for each of these six areas—mission, goals, roles, priorities, communication, and management—but you must also be as succinct as possible. The goal of the CX Charter is to have a document that summarizes the intent and parameters of your CX initiative in a form that will not be off-putting to potential team members. The message that needs to shine through is excitement and opportunity—come join us!

CONCLUSION

You have a CX Mission Statement. You have a CX Success Blueprint. And you have a CX Charter. From the aspirational to the theoretical to the logistical, you are now equipped to take your organization into its customer-first era.

What now? If it isn't clear yet, I'll be explicit: You have a long, exciting road ahead. Start with baby steps.

Customer experience is a way of life for you and your organization, it is the motivating cause behind forward- and inward-facing decisions big and small, it is the secret weapon behind recruiting and retaining employees, and it is the key to seeing your customers through their entire journey with you. Nothing that important is ever going to be easy. A customer experience mindset may feel like a headwind if your organization is in need of drastic change, but it will become the wind in your sails once the mechanics are in place and buy-in from the full organizational hierarchy is complete. Remember, you are leading a strategy, not simply measuring feedback.

- Carry your CX Mission Statement in your heart. This is your *why*.

CONCLUSION

- Create a results-focused CX strategy to take the right actions and gain that all-important leadership buy-in for your efforts.
- Keep in touch with your customers through both regular feedback programs and tools like customer journey mapping.
- Continue to engage cross-functional support and to help everyone understand that they are on the CX team with a CX Charter.
- When in doubt, think of the customer. What are they really trying to do? You are helping someone live their life with more freedom, more success, or simply more ease. That's no small thing!

As you sit down to write your first CX Mission Statement, try to be present to the task even as you look forward to what lies ahead: the CX Success Blueprint, the granular journey mapping, your buy-in and recruiting efforts around the organization, and the CX Charter. I hope you look forward to the activities as much as you look forward to the results. Most of all, I hope you look forward to being part of an organizational culture that prides itself on creating and delivering what matters most for those they serve.

Thanks for fighting the good fight on behalf of your customer. You've got this!

WHAT'S NEXT?

MOMENTUM STARTS WITH ONE INTENTIONAL ACTION—AND you're already on your way by picking up this book. Keep the energy going with tools, inspiration, and guidance to help you turn purpose into progress and progress into lasting impact.

Your next great experience starts now. Come see us at www.experienceiseverythingbook.com. Here's a shortcut:

See you there,
Jeannie

NOTES

1 Fred Reichheld, *Winning on Purpose: The Unbeatable Strategy of Loving Customers* (Harvard Business Review Press, 2021).
2 Shar VanBoskirk et al., "State of Customer Obsession, 2023," Forrester, October 1, 2023, https://www.forrester.com/report/the-state-of-customer-obsession-2023/RES179912.

ONE LAST THING...

YOU WON'T BE ABLE TO DO IT ALL. And that's not a failure! It's simply reality.

Customer experience lives at the intersection of human needs and business constraints. Budgets are real. Time is limited. Tradeoffs are inevitable. Even the most committed leaders must balance what customers want with what organizations can deliver.

The goal was never perfection. The goal is progress.

So here's my request: **Start somewhere.**

Customer experience isn't one initiative or one department's responsibility. It's the cumulative effect of how people think, decide, and act—day after day. That's why mindset, strategy, and discipline matter so much. They give you something steady to return to when everything feels complex or overwhelming.

Your mission reminds people why the work matters.

Your strategy helps you focus on what will matter most right now.

Your discipline keeps the work alive through busy days and shifting priorities.

ONE LAST THING . . .

This isn't a checklist to complete. They're supports you can lean on (some more than the others) as you move forward.

You don't have to wait until everything is perfectly clear or aligned. You begin by making one intentional choice.

Decide what "good" looks like— before something goes wrong.

Too many organizations wait until customers are frustrated or trust is already eroding before aligning internally. Staying ahead means doing the opposite.

Define expectations when things are calm, so teams aren't scrambling when they're not.

Align on how you'll show up when systems fail. Or when customers are confused. Or when emotions run high.

This is where mission becomes practical and strategy becomes visible. Prepared teams don't just react faster, they recover better. And recovery, handled well, is often where trust is built.

Start with one moment that matters.

Pick an interaction that customers experience every day. Focus on one that quietly reinforces your mission. The moment that either delivers on your promise or subtly undermines it.

Improve that moment.
Clarify it.
Humanize it.

ONE LAST THING . . .

When strategy helps you choose which moments matter most, small changes add up quickly. These small wins, repeated consistently, create the outcomes leaders care about most.

Say the quiet part out loud.
Customers don't expect perfection. They expect clarity.
Tell them what's happening.
Tell them what to expect next.
Tell them what you're doing to help.

Clear communication is a discipline. It reduces effort, builds confidence, and turns uncertainty into understanding. When communication is intentional, even imperfect experiences can feel respectful and trustworthy.

Build one habit—not a program.
You don't need another initiative. You need one practice your team can keep.
Start meetings with a real customer story focused on your mission.
Ask consistent questions about customer friction points.
Create a simple rhythm for reviewing what you've learned and deciding what to do next.
Habits are how experience becomes culture. They're how good intentions turn into reliable behavior, and momentum survives competing priorities.

Stay curious longer than feels comfortable.
When the data surprises you, resist the urge to explain it away. When feedback stings, pause before defending. Ask one more question. Listen one layer deeper.

Curiosity keeps your mindset open and your strategy relevant. It helps you stay ahead of customers' expectations, before they tell you you've fallen behind.

Progress beats perfection.
Customer experience doesn't improve because everything is perfectly designed. It improves because leaders are willing to act, reflect, adjust, and act again.

Start small.
Learn fast.
Stay committed.

Customer experience isn't a project you finish. It's a capability you build.

Every intentional moment.
Every clear decision.
Every disciplined habit.

They compound.
Start where you are.
Stay human.
Keep going.

Because experience isn't everything all at once. **It's everything, built one moment at a time.**

CXI Navigator Framework